Vanished Peoples

Vanished Peoples

The Archaic
Dorset &
Beothuk People
of Newfoundland

PETER SUCH

NC Press Limited, Toronto, 1978

Cover designed by Mel Johnston.

Canadian Cataloguing in Publication Data

Such, Peter, 1939–
    Vanished peoples

Bibliography: p.
Includes index.
ISBN 0–919600–84–0 bd.   ISBN 0–919600–83–2 pa.

I. Indians of North America — Newfoundland.
I. Title.

E78.N72S83   970'.004'97   C77–001/21–5

The SI units and symbols used in the text of *Vanished Peoples* have been
reviewed by the Canadian Government Specifications Board and are found to
comply with the requirements of the two National Standards of Canada —
the International System of Units (SI) CAN3–Z234.2–74 and the Canadian Metric
Practice Guide CAN3–Z234.1–76.

We would like to thank the Ontario Arts Council and the Canada Council
for their assistance in the production of this book.

New Canada Publications,
a division of NC Press Limited
Box 4010, Terminal A,
Toronto, Ontario, Canada.

Contents

Acknowledgements

A book of this kind is really the work of many scholars over many decades. Very little of it is original. Essentially, I have put together the research of archaeologists, ethnographers, historians and other experts, to present as clear a picture as presently possible of the aboriginal history of Newfoundland. I was led into *Vanished Peoples* by the research for my novel *Riverrun* (1973).

Since that time Prof. James Tuck of Memorial University has published *Newfoundland and Labrador Prehistory* (1976), without which the sections on the Maritime Archaic and Cape Dorset would have been almost impossible to write. It is a beautiful publication by the National Museum of Man and I would encourage those interested in further archaeological research to obtain it.

The final sections owe much to J. P. Howley's *The Beothuk or Red Indians of Newfoundland,* a formerly rare compendium published in 1915, which has been recently reissued as a Coles Canadiana reprint. Professor Helen Devereux of Laurentian University, a pioneer in Beothuk archaeology, allowed me to use her unpublished thesis on Beothuk sites as well as giving me initial encouragement.

The valuable publications on related matters are listed in the Bibliography. To their authors, my thanks. Especially valuable were those by Dr. Urve Linnamae, Dr. Elmer Harp Jr., Department of Anthropology, Dartmouth College, New Hampshire; Dr. Robert McGhee, Arctic Archaeologist for the Museum of Man; and Donald MacLeod, Archaeologist for the Ontario Government. These last two scholars have given me so much help and advice, so many times beyond the scope of their publications, that they really deserve co-authorship.

During the final stages of the manuscript they, as well as Prof. Devereux, Drs. James Tuck and Edmund Carpenter, were kind enough to read it on short notice and to offer many valuable suggestions.

James Thistle, Chief Cataloguer for the Newfoundland Museum supplied the maps of archaeological sites. In addition he made it possible to photograph many items under his care and supplied the editors with additional illustrative material.

Lastly, I must acknowledge the tremendous cooperation and encouragement of the Museum of Man in Ottawa, through James Wright, Head of the Research Section of the Archaeological Survey of Canada and through its Director, Dr. Wm. Taylor Jr., who initiated the Museum's Beothuk project in 1964. All of the above-mentioned contributed to the book's illustrations. Rita Dudzisz, Canadian Studies secretary of Atkinson College, sped the book on its way by typing its many versions.

This is for my daughter Luba Such, who was there, and for Wendy Campbell.

Colour Plates

I. The burial mound at L'Anse Amour.

Reprinted, by permission, from Robert McGhee, *The Burial at L'Anse Amour,* p. 13, 1977 by the National Museums of Canada.

II. Artifacts from the Port au Choix cemetery.

At the top is an antler comb carved in the shape of a duck. The duck's beak points towards a toggling harpoon point, and a small barbed sealing harpoon head is below the comb's "tail." A barbed fishspear point in the centre of the picture has a gouge to the right and a grey slate ground bayonet and lance point to the left. The two amethyst crystals come from a medicine man's pouch and are often found randomly in Archaic sites. Reprinted, by permission, from James A. Tuck, *Newfoundland and Labrador Prehistory,* colour plate I, p. 18, 1976 by the National Museums of Canada.

III. Swallowtailed pendants and a Dorset stylized bear.

As anthropologist Edmund Carpenter asserts, Beothuk swallowtail pendants sometimes have an amazing similarity to Newfoundland Dorset amulets, such as this stylized bear in the centre over the 25 cent piece.

IV. The Beaches Site.

Stretching across an arm of the sea in Alexander Bay, the Beaches is one of the most productive archaeological areas in Newfoundland. Formed by sandy gravel bars which stretch like causeways between two islands and the mainland, this area has been sinking since it was inhabited by the Maritime Archaic nearly five thousand years ago.

V. Epaves Bay from L'Anse aux Meadows.

Where Norse ships landed a thousand years ago near the tip of Newfoundland. Courtesy *Canadian Geographic Journal*. Photograph by Birgitta Wallace for Parks Canada.

Photographs page 28 courtesy *Eberhard Otto Photography Limited,* 32 Vicora Linkway, Don Mills, Ontario, M3C 1B1.

Preface

Canada does not have any extraordinary monuments left by great Empires. In the past, except for a few pioneers, Canadian archaeologists directed most of their attention to foreign parts earning for themselves a well-deserved international reputation in such far-flung places as Egypt, Turkey, Africa and South America. But, increasingly, through the work of our National Museum and our Universities, Canadian archaeologists have been directing their attention homewards. The results have been fascinating. Although there are few great temples of past grandeur, Canadian archaeology has begun painstakingly to discover the roots of man's culture in the New World, piecing together a story of great migrations and ways of life that help our understanding of how this continent was first settled and developed.

From the Yukon, where Dr. William Irving has found remains of the continent's first immigrants, to Ontario and Newfoundland where Donald MacLeod, Prof. Helen Devereux, Dr. McGhee and Dr. Tuck and many others have illuminated the ways of life and the final days of these pioneer stone-age peoples, a picture has emerged of Canada as the key to many unanswered questions about North America and its native peoples.

My own interest has been to keep in touch with the work of these experts over the years, much of it still unpublished, particularly as to how it relates to the Native Peoples of Newfoundland. Such things as actually unearthing with the tip of my digging trowel a beautifully made large stone point thousands of years old, or of being a member of a small survey team suddenly discovering an unknown French fort in the bush near Hudson's Bay have fuelled my sense of being in touch with my own country's ancestral past and helping in a small way to discover it.

We all need a sense of our past, of how our present and indeed our future grow out of it. To see ourselves as part of that continuing tradition as it keeps evolving and not separate from it is really the main aim of this book.

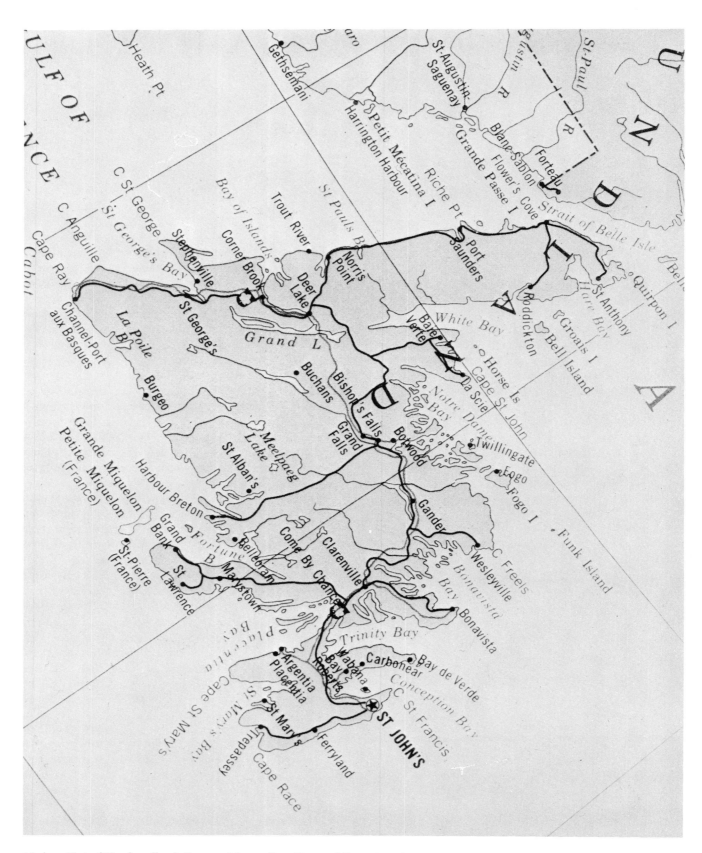

Modern Map of Newfoundland. Courtesy Metropolitan Toronto Library Board.

Chapter I

The Leading Edge

Seven thousand five hundred years ago, near present-day L'Anse-Amour on the south coast of Labrador, a group of stone-age hunters and fishermen finished piling a heap of boulders over the ceremonial pit where they had buried a 13-year-old boy. It had been a lot of work, scooping out the sandy soil so that, standing on the damp floor of the pit, a man could not even see over the edge. There had to be enough room to move about in there, to light the ceremonial fires, one on each side, and to lay the boy down between them.

After the ceremony they left him face down, head turned to the west, sewn in bark covering. They smeared everything used in the ceremony with red paint. They had left the paint-stones and the deer-horn pestle, with which they had ground and applied the magic paint, by the boy's side. By his head, each had placed a spearpoint or knife of chipped flint or polished bone. Two spearpoints were put by his left shoulder. In front of his face was the ivory tusk from a walrus they had killed. As though the boy had been a walrus himself, they had left the harpoon head they had used under his body, attached to the line, with its knotted end running through the toggle-handle. One held onto this when an animal made its mad rush and the line stretched taut.

When he died, the boy had his decorated bone pendant around his neck, and also his hollow bird-bone flute.

Filling the pit in again was a big job. First they put a stone slab on the boy's back and covered everything with sand, then they marked the way the body lay with stones standing on edge. Finally they carried boulders from all around and made a big pile of them.

When Canadian archaeologists James Tuck and Robert McGhee, from Memorial University, found the boy's skeleton face-down they were astonished. Of all the ways people were buried in ages past, only very rarely were they laid in the earth face-down. Never before had they seen such a thing on this continent and never before in the graves common to these people. Was the boy a sacrificial victim, they wondered? Perhaps he had been ritually strangled to appease some powerful god. A heavy stone slab had been put on the boy's back. Was that to keep his soul, angry at being sacrificed, from rising in revenge to haunt his people?

No one will ever know. But we can imagine those stone-age hunters, finishing their arduous task and looking up over the narrow strait to present-day Newfoundland. They had not yet crossed that Strait of Belle Isle but their descendants would. And when they did, they would be the first people ever to land on the northern tip of that rocky peninsula. Newfoundland was the last place in North America still uninhabited. It was also the place where, nearly 6 000 years later, the Europeans, perhaps the Irish, most likely the Vikings, would make their landfall in what was, to us, the New World.

Those who buried this boy were an ancient people who were part of the Maritime Archaic tool tradition. Earliest traces of them in Southern Labrador go back approximately 9 000 years, thousands of years before the Egyptians thought to build their pyramids.

Where these archaic peoples originally came from is a question still not conclusively answered. But they spread out to nearly every part of the continent. The most likely theory is that they had evolved, with the change of climate and hunting conditions, from an earlier people, the "Paleo" or "Dawn Age" Indians, about whom we know very little.

These earliest people, the first inhabitants of the Americas probably came from Asia. They had been gradually pushed out by the huge lobe of ice that ground its way deep into the Asian continent during the last ice age, 25–40 000 years ago. Those who drifted west reached present-day Europe; those who came east, the Americas.

For many years archaeologists have speculated that the Paleo-Indians' ancestors came to North America across the Bering Land Bridge. Although the glaciers, three kilometres and more high in some places, were pushing down into Canada, geologists say that there was a narrow corridor between the two lobes of ice. It ran across the middle of Alaska, down through the Yukon and into the foothills of the Rockies.

As the ice receded and advanced, waves of many now-extinct animals followed this route, including huge woolly mammoths, spruce-eating mastodons, dangerous sabre-toothed tigers, and beavers eight times the size of those today. There was plenty to eat for the courageous hunter.

And hunt them these hardy wanderers did. In 1975, Prof. William Irving and his assistants from the University of Toronto discovered, near Old Crow in the Yukon, the weapons of these early people and the remains of the huge animals they killed. Finally, after years of searching, there was proof that people had come into North America this way. It was one of the most exciting finds of contemporary archaeology. The next year Irving's expedition unearthed a fossilized human jawbone more than 20 000 years old.

Many scientists believed that these hunters helped to exterminate the big game of those times. It's even thought they may have killed off the early horse.

Wandering down this unglaciated corridor, the Paleo-Indians found their way to the tip of South America. Then, 10 000 years ago, the glaciers began to retreat. Rivers and streams gushed abundantly from their blue edges and new forests sprang up in the washed-out soils that had been entombed by the ice. By now the big game had gone, but smaller game such as deer and caribou abounded in the freshly-minted land.

The Paleo-Indians hunted with new weapons of better design and, in these new conditions, probably evolved into the people we call the "Archaic." Knots of these Archaic people tied themselves to places where they could develop more specialized ways of life. Over the thousands of years, they stayed to fish or hunt and forgot even the languages of their distant cousins who were still living much in their old way. Some of these fragments of the Archaic core group may have evolved into the tribes we recognize today.

One group of Paleo-Indians began to live mostly by the sea and became a "Maritime Archaic" people who buried the boy and looked across to the empty island of Newfoundland. They were close cousins to the Paleo-Indians who still hunted in the interior of Nova Scotia where they had drifted, two thousand years before.

The glaciers which had covered Labrador had barely started to melt when these Maritime Archaic people moved onto the rocky coasts. The interior of Labrador was not completely free of ice until six thousand years ago. Harsh land even now, the interior was not settled, and then very sparsely, until about fifteen hundred years ago. The settlers were people who had lived exclusively by hunting on the Canadian shield. Called the "Shield Archaic," they may have become the Montagnais and Naskapi of the present day. Most of their time, the Maritime Archaic spent near the coast, sealing in spring, catching fish, harpooning sea mammals and, especially, spearing salmon in the rivers. Once winter closed down in earnest, they went inland to hunt caribou.

They were a hardy, adaptable people whose hunting kit was quite practical and not very elaborate. "No nonsense" technology, as it has been described by Don MacLeod, Government of Ontario Archaeologist.

From the skeletons that have been found, they were a healthy race, although perhaps half the children died soon after birth, if we count the numbers buried at the Port au Choix cemetery in Newfoundland. Only the fittest survived. Tooth decay was almost unknown although those people found in Port au Choix, who had lived to a fairly ripe age, had teeth that were very worn down, in some cases to the pulp, from a hearty diet with lots of roughage.

In the rough and tumble of hunting over rugged terrain, bones broke frequently but mended on their own. A tough people. From these burials, too, we can guess that their basic social unit was the extended family. They lived without chiefs or formal authority except, perhaps, a shaman, an expert in magic.

For a few thousand years the Maritime Archaic flourished on Labrador's coasts.

Then, from the high Arctic, about 4 500 years, ago, an ancient race called Paleo-Eskimos began expanding into their territory. With changes in the weather, from cold to more temperate times and back again, the meeting point of these two groups probably shifted northwards, then southwards. The Eskimos depended much on the sea. Their skill at hunting seal on pack-ice through the seals' breathing holes meant they were better able to assert a claim to the coastal settlements year round than the Maritime Archaic who moved south to more temperate climes.

About the same time, or perhaps somewhat earlier some of the Maritime Archaic moved across the Strait of Belle Isle into uninhabited Newfoundland, leaving behind their relatives in Labrador.

Skeleton of boy found in L'Anse-Amour burial mound.

Face-down, a heavy stone slab on his back, lying in a ceremonial pit one and a half meters deep, was this boy a sacrificial victim? He is buried with a litter of spearpoints and other hunting tools. Courtesy National Museum, Robert McGhee, The Burial at L'Anse-Amour.

An extraordinary cultural exchange seems to have taken place between these two peoples. It was previously thought that the early Eskimos had invented the principle of a toggling harpoon head that opened up inside the animal. But the discovery of the harpoon head in the young boy's grave, put there 7 500 years ago, proved that the Maritime Archaic people had used such a device thousands of years before. This harpoon is now thought to be the oldest toggling sea mammal hunting equipment found anywhere in the world. It was probably the Eskimos who borrowed the idea from the Maritime Archaic, and made good use of it!

On the other hand, it was always thought the bow and arrow was invented by the early Indians. Recent discoveries seem to cast doubt on this as well. Some of the tiny projectile points characteristic of the early Eskimos were clearly arrowheads. The wooden shafts of bows and arrows rot completely and so have never been found. About the time these two groups met on the coasts of Labrador, the Maritime Archaic people seem to have started making, for the first time, the same kind of stone arrow heads. Many of these arrow heads and other stone tools were made of a distinctive kind of stone found only in Northern Labrador. Called Ramah Chert, it seems to have been traded between these two groups, and widely through North America.

Some artifacts found in the L'Anse-Amour burial.

A flute made from a hollow bird-bone, a small bone pendant decorated with fine nicks, and a piece of antler used to grind and apply the red paint used in the ceremonial burial are the oldest organic materials fashioned by man found in Labrador and Newfoundland. The other materials are graphite paintstones. Courtesy National Museum, Robert McGhee, L'Anse-Amour.

Chapter II

The First Newfoundlanders:
The Maritime Archaic

The island the Maritime Archaic moved into 5 000 years ago was an unusual one. Only half the species of the animals that inhabited the mainland had found sanctuary in the new lakes and the forests that had grown as the ice receded. Then, as now, there were no snakes, no reptiles of any kind, no amphibians. Even today there are only scattered pockets of frogs which were brought over by white men in the late eighteenth century. There were no porcupines or squirrels.

The caribou came with their delicate antlers reaching like hands, but not the moose. These larger browsers were introduced in 1929 for the benefit of modern hunters. Today caribou are relatively rare.

Lynx came too, but not their natural prey, the snowshoe hare. Newfoundland lynx, adapting the habits of larger cats, culled the sick and old from caribou herds. Hunting in pairs, the male leapt between the antlers and scratched at the beast's eyes to blind it, while the female snaked in to attack its vital parts.

Caribou on the mainland roamed the northern woods and the tundra, the barren lands, in well-defined herds that could easily be followed for food, clothing and shelter. Newfoundland caribou found it necessary to browse over a much wider area, resembling their mainland cousins only in the fall, the rutting season, when they congregated into larger herds for their annual migration down from Newfoundland's rocky northern peninsula. They returned singly in the spring.

Wolves glided silver among the birches until the last one was shot at Gaff Topsails in 1911. Beaver and otter swam the inland waters, sable and marten nosed through the bushlands and, in the fall, the trees were thick with ptarmigan, a special Newfoundland variety that changes colour with the seasons. The explorer John Cartwright remarks of them in 1768, "They became in cold weather so tame as to appear deficient in

the principle of self-preservation; so that they are killed at pleasure, and may be reckoned as a kind of domestic poultry to the Indians." On Funk and Fogo islands, vast colonies of sea-birds, including the now extinct Great Auk, rested and laid millions of eggs.

There was also the incredible richness of the sea itself where the Gulf and Labrador currents meet. Salmon spurted in vivid runs up foaming rivers in late summer. Seal, ten times more numerous than today, played in bays filled with islands, barked and rolled on headlands and beaches. Whales and dolphins plunged and dived. Mackerel flashed in troughs of waves over deepfeeding cod, and schools of knifeblade herrings dashed across the shallows. Occasionally a polar bear, stranded on his iceberg, would angrily drift into harbour.

But, rich as it sounds, Newfoundland was not an easy place to live in for these Maritime Archaic people. Besides a savage climate, particularly in the north, there was little soil on which an agricultural community could develop and very little in the way of natural edible vegetation. Many and various as the other food resources were, no single one of them was available year round in one location. Newfoundland straddles many distinct ecological zones belonging to none of them — an "ecotone" area.

As part of a delicate ecological balance, the Archaic peoples had to keep moving to survive. They had to develop different skills and techniques for each kind of game. They could not afford to be over-specialized like those Indian tribes who had reliable food resources around which they could develop a more sophisticated culture. This is perhaps why, in the Gulf areas and North Eastern America generally, the Archaic group gives way only much later to more specialized kinds of lifestyles like those further south and west. At certain times of the year, these first inhabitants of Newfoundland had to use the skills of the Eskimo, at others the techniques of the salmon fishers

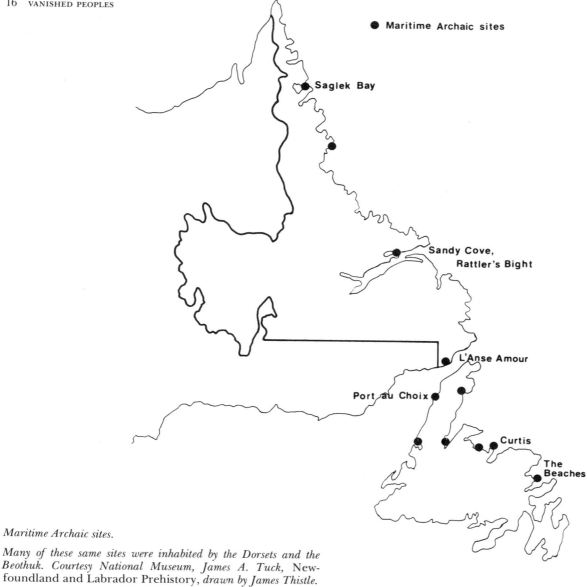

● Maritime Archaic sites

●Saglek Bay

●Sandy Cove,
Rattler's Bight

●L'Anse Amour

Port au Choix●

Curtis

The
Beaches

Maritime Archaic sites.

Many of these same sites were inhabited by the Dorsets and the Beothuk. Courtesy National Museum, James A. Tuck, Newfoundland and Labrador Prehistory, *drawn by James Thistle.*

of the mainland, at still others, they had to become caribou hunters or trappers.

The sea, however, was the most abundant, most easily exploited resource, and therefore the most tempting (as it later proved to be for Western Europeans). Thus, in Newfoundland, the Archaic people seem to have relied most on sea-mammal hunting. The caribou was of secondary importance, as was salmon.

One of their caribou-hunting campsites was in the Exploits River valley, the valley which became, in later times, the final refuge of the Beothuk. Other traces of Maritime Archaic habitation have been found around Twillingate Island and also at the Beaches archaeo-

logical site in Bonavista Bay which, so far, seems the oldest.

The only other large Maritime Archaic site found on the island is at Port au Choix. It has been investigated over several years by Dr. Elmer Harp and Prof. James Tuck. It was probably a sacred cemetery because there is evidence to show that some of the ninety people buried here were brought here for burial purposes some time after they had died.

Fortunately, these people were buried with many of their tools and household goods so that archaeologists have a good idea how they lived, despite the fact that only the hard materials have remained.

A Newfoundland caribou.

An important food resource for early Newfoundlanders, the caribou were hunted at favourite crossing points in their annual migration *southwards by the Maritime Archaic and the Dorsets. Courtesy D. MacLeod.*

Most of the hunting weapons were ground and polished slate spears or lances. Hafted to wooden shafts, these would be ideal to finish off sea-mammals that had been caught by toggling or barbed harpoons. There were fishspears with barbed stone points, and various kinds of scrapers for preparing hides. In addition there were awls for pushing holes into leather or other materials to sew them together and some very finely-made sewing needles with tiny holes which suggest these early people did some very delicate needlework.

Many bird beaks, animal skulls, claws and teeth were found with the people buried at Port au Choix,

suggesting that these objects had religious significance for the Maritime Archaic. The powers of these animals — their swiftness, fierceness, courage or cunning — would have been revered by a hunting people. The possession of these amulets would ensure the wearer magical protection or imbue him with some of the animal's special powers. Combs, whistles and pendants were also made, as well as a few art objects. Probably the clothes the people wore were decorative, and shell necklaces and bone pendants were used as jewelry. One of the few objects resembling modern sculpture was a very simplified image of a killer whale.

Maritime Archaic stone tools.

The axe or adze head is stained with red ochre. The tiny stone points were probably arrowheads, the larger one is a broken knifeblade.

What is most striking about these burials, however, is that red ochre was smeared over everything as well as the body. This red powdery pigment appears to have had religious significance for these people as it did, we shall see later, for the Beothuk.

For probably more than a thousand years, the Maritime Archaic had the island to themselves, without competition from the early Eskimos who were gradually taking over from the Maritime Archaic's relatives in Labrador. Archaeological evidence indicates that the Maritime Archaic were disappearing from Labrador's coasts about 3 000 years ago although some may have survived a little longer by changing mainly to caribou hunting.

The Paleo-Eskimos replaced these Maritime Archaic peoples in Labrador. Then, by 1500–2000 years ago, a late form of Paleo-Eskimos called the Dorsets were thriving on Newfoundland's coasts, occupying most of the Maritime Archaic's sites.

At first it was thought the Maritime Archaic had simply vanished and that the Dorsets had settled in their place. We have no evidence of any conflict between them and it is hard to imagine a people who had lived in Newfoundland so long simply dying out. Now archaeologists think that the Maritime Archaic, pushed from their usual coastal sites, found others. Instead of moving inland only for short periods to hunt caribou, they may have been forced to become even more nomadic, spending most of their time in the interior, foraging on the coast whenever they had the chance.

Elsewhere on the continent, away from the sea, Archaic peoples had survived without going to the sea: varying the tools they used and the animals they hunted according to the seasons and the areas they found themselves in.

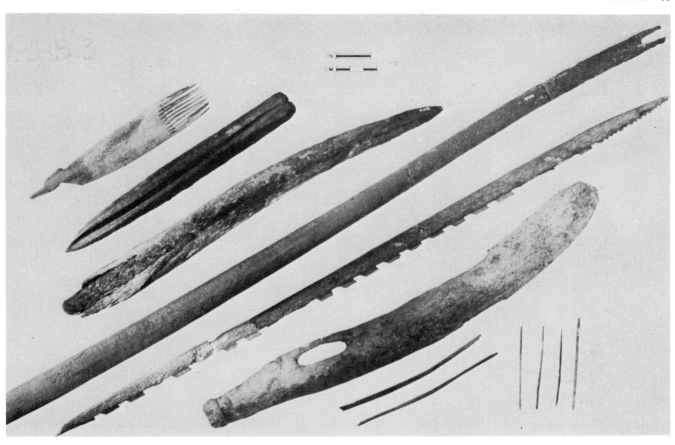

Maritime Archaic Bone Implements.

Top left is duck-shaped comb and below it a grooved awl. The walrus tusk dagger, below the awl, may have fitted into the antler-bone sheath above the needles. A cord or belt could have been passed through the hole at the top of the sheath. Running diagonally across the picture is a whale-bone harpoon foreshaft and below it a barbed fishing spear or leister. Courtesy Don MacLeod.

Digging for artifacts at the Beaches site.

A short period of unusually low tide uncovers a rich assortment of Maritime Archaic stone tools.

Ground slate lances of the Maritime Archaic.

These bayonets were probably used to finish off large sea-mammals that were first harpooned.

It is possible that the Maritime Archaic in Newfoundland survived in the interior as the Shield Archaic did, for the few hundred years that they seem to have vanished.

It is important to remember that archaeological sites are found mostly by accident and only patient work over decades can confirm educated guesses. Perhaps Maritime Archaic sites of this period, with clearly dateable materials like charcoal from fires, are still to be found. Perhaps they have been drowned and washed away in the past hundred years, as loggers raised and lowered the levels of the lakes on whose shores the settlements stood. The only thing we can say with surety is that the sites occupied on the coasts by the Maritime Archaic people were taken over by an artistic Eskimo race who themselves vanished from Newfoundland only a short time before the Vikings landed at L'Anse aux Meadows.

Maritime Archaic amulets from the Port au Choix cemetery. Two are of birds; one is a human effigy. Courtesy Newfoundland Museum.

Natural concretions buried in gravesites at Port au Choix by the Maritime Archaic. Unusually shaped natural objects such as these were probably considered magical. Courtesy Newfoundland Museum.

Sculpture of a killer whale found at Port au Choix.
Courtesy Newfoundland Museum.

Chapter III

The First Invaders: The Dorset

The Dorset Eskimos were once lords of a huge Arctic territory stretching from Victoria Island in the West, all the way across to Greenland and down through Labrador to Newfoundland.

These Eskimos left their remains over this vast area beginning almost 3 000 years ago and continuing until as late as two hundred years before the Cabots landed in Newfoundland. Newfoundland, the furthest south they penetrated, went through a cold period from A.D. 300 to 700 making the island more of an arctic zone than it is today. It was during this cold time that the Dorset flourished in Newfoundland and the Maritime Archaic seemed to disappear.

Travelling was not easy for these people. Unlike modern Eskimos, the Dorset may not at first have had boats. They may have crossed the twelve kilometres to Newfoundland across the Strait of Belle Isle on the thick pack-ice. Although they had sleds, they had no dogs to help pull them. The first dogsleds appear later with the Thule Eskimos. Straining in the traces of sleds piled with their goods, and perhaps their children, along the treacherous shifting coastal ice, these people soon spread to nearly every corner of the island, finding the well-chosen places where the Maritime Archaic had lived: Port au Choix, Twillingate, and the Beaches, for instance.

These sites may have been abandoned by the Maritime Archaic in the dead of the unusually cold winters when the Dorsets first ventured upon them. They may have squatted there, dug pits for the low walls of their skin-tent houses, and set out to keep body and soul together by venturing onto the rubbery ice with which they were so familiar, but which lasted only half as long here as in their Arctic homeland.

Compared to their more established relatives in the Arctic heartland, and even the newer settlements of Labrador, these Newfoundland Dorsets were pioneers, straining to survive at the edge of their natural territory. They were used to crouching stealthily by the tell-tale mounds of blowholes, waiting patiently for the seal to poke its nose up to breathe, and jamming down hard and straight with the harpoon.

On the flimsier ice off Newfoundland, that kind of hunting didn't work. But, luckily, there were thousands upon thousands of harp seals whelping on the drift ice in spring. Ninety percent of the bones found in one of their garbage dumps at Port au Choix were seal bones. How much the Dorsets must have relied on these animals for food!

That the Dorsets stuck pretty well to the coasts seems clear from their remains, although these camps might not have been used year round. At only one small campsite, Pope's Point on the Exploits River, where the caribou crossed, do we know that they ventured far inland. This, in later times, was the heartland of the Beothuk.

Is it possible that the Maritime Archaic, shunning conflict as the Beothuk always did in later times, simply accommodated to the presence of the Dorset? The Maritime Archaic living off caribou, fishing the long interior lakes, would move to other places on the seashore. The Dorsets would stay mostly on the coasts. During these colder years, the sealing was probably exceptionally good: the ice more trustworthy.

Did these peoples borrow, steal, or find each other's gear? They may have learned from each other. There is evidence that the Dorsets of Newfoundland changed the shape of some of their tools slightly. And, as we'll see later, their distinctive harpoon, greatly developed and refined from the early Paleo-Eskimo model, was borrowed in turn by the Beothuk.

Many of the Dorset tools found in Newfoundland were made differently from those used by the Dorsets still living in the high Arctic. They were, in some cases, ground more extensively than those of their cousins in the Arctic, a technique the Maritime Archaic were fond of. There were different materials at

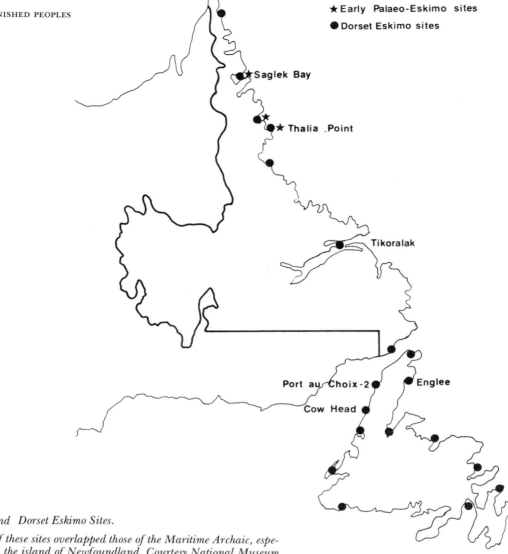

★ Early Palaeo-Eskimo sites
● Dorset Eskimo sites

Saglek Bay

Thalia .Point

Tikoralak

Port au Choix-2

Englee

Cow Head

Paleo and Dorset Eskimo Sites.

Many of these sites overlapped those of the Maritime Archaic, especially in the island of Newfoundland. Courtesy National Museum of Man, James A. Tuck, Newfoundland and Labrador Prehistory, *drawn by James Thistle.*

hand in Newfoundland which may account for these differences. But perhaps these minute similarities, discernible only to trained archaeologists, are evidence that the Maritime Archaic still existed, and influenced the Dorsets.

There were other differences. In the Arctic, the Dorsets used seal-oil lamps to light and heat their dwellings. In Newfoundland these lamps are rare. Instead, the Dorsets built wood fires in stonelined hearths running down the middle of their houses, very much like eighteenth century Laplanders' houses. The availability of wood for such a splendid blaze must have been a luxury these pioneers were pleased to find. That the sun did not disappear in the dead of winter made a lamp unnecessary.

Urve Linnamae has shown that Newfoundland Dorset soapstone vessels, used for storage and cooking, had more steeply-angled sides than those used by the Dorsets in the Arctic. A nesting set of these pots, from tiny to very large, was found in Newfoundland. Perhaps the steeper sides were developed so that the stone pots would fit more easily inside each other for carrying.

Early drawing of the interior of a Laplander house.

Dorset houses found in Newfoundland seemed to have a similar central hearth cutting the floor in two.

Dorset Housepits.

These 600–700 year old Dorset houses on Sugluk Island in northern Quebec are being excavated by an Eskimo crew; the ancestors of those who displaced the Dorsets. The house depressions are being dug in a grid of one and a half metres, separated by unexcavated walls, a common archaeological technique. Courtesy Dr. William Taylor, as published in Six Chapters of Canada's Pre-History *by J. V. Wright, the National Museum of Man, Ottawa.*

Dorset amulets from Newfoundland.

These may have been tied to weapon shafts for good luck. Courtesy National Museum of Man, James A. Tuck, Newfoundland Labrador Prehistory.

Dorset soapstone dish or pot.

In Newfoundland these were made with more steeply angled sides than in the Arctic. This would make for easier "nesting" of one inside the other. Courtesy Newfoundland Museum.

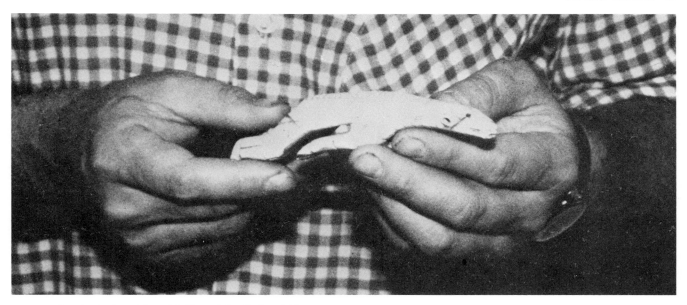

Arctic archaeologist Dr. Robert McGhee of the National Museum of Man holds a "floating bear" carved approximately 2 000 years ago in the Arctic. Probably in an attempt to depict both the "insides" and "outsides" of the bear, these carvings are incised with lines suggesting the internal skeleton. Hollowed out underneath, some of these bears have been found "plugged" with wood. These kinds of powerful, probably religious, carvings were not made by the Newfoundland branch of the Dorsets.

Epoxy casts being made of Dorset carvings.

Swimming in a plaster sea are a tiny polar bear, whale and a bear's head. These copies will be made available to Canadian museums.

Separated from the heartland of their culture, the Dorsets of Newfoundland seem to have lost much of that complex religion which, in the Arctic, had expressed itself in very well-made carvings. This pioneer society did not leave behind nearly the same number or quality of finely-carved objects. The extraordinary polar bears, seal, Arctic fowl, and the human figures with their distinct high-raised parka collars, found by archaeologists in the Arctic, were not produced by these pioneer Dorsets of Newfoundland.

Although the Newfoundland Dorsets continued to decorate their harpoon heads, which by this time had quite distinctive sharp stone blades slotted into their ends, only about one percent of the stone, bone and ivory objects found on the island could be counted as figurative carvings.

Did the fact that these people in the southern climate of Newfoundland had no long unbroken winter nights to spend carving account for this? Most of the Newfoundland carvings are not made "in the round" but tend to be more easily-made flat pendants or amulets.

In the Arctic, the art objects which seem to be connected with formal religious practices, are mostly of human or bear forms, the latter, the greatest "helping spirit," or combinations of human and animal shapes.

In Newfoundland, there are practically no human or animal-human forms and very few larger carvings. Dr. Elmer Harp Jr. has shown, from a study of their work, that most Newfoundland Dorset carvings are amulets whose function was attached to hunting magic like the objects used by the Maritime Archaic. Could it be that the "no nonsense" practical hunting magic of the Maritime Archaic influenced the Newfoundland Dorset to abandon their old religion?

Interestingly, the Dorset seal images from Newfoundland nearly all have a raised head. This is the harp seal on Newfoundland pack-ice, head lifted to observe the hunter, not the Arctic image of the seal with head straight forward as if pushing up into a blowhole or swimming through the water.

As the climate warmed up, did the sealing decline? By the years A.D. 700 to 800, the Dorsets were dwindling rapidly. Did they try to struggle back across the Belle Isle Strait to Labrador? Were they the legendary Skraelings the Vikings of the Vinland Sagas fought so desperately? Could it be that the last band of Dorset, a thousand years after their forefathers invaded the island, were finally expelled from it by the Vikings' iron weapons? Or did the Dorset run into stiffening competition from inhabitants in the interior who were perhaps descended from the supposedly extinct Maritime Archaic?

Dorset toggling harpoon head. The foreshaft is ivory. Side blades would have been inserted in the holes of the head itself, through which also ran the line. Courtesy Newfoundland Museum.

Dorset bear heads.

The three stylized ones come from Newfoundland and appear to be self-contained amulets, perhaps worn on clothing or attached to hunting weapons. The upper four, however, come from Abverdjar, near Igloolik, and appear to have been cut from complete effigies. Courtesy Eskimo Realities, *Edmund Carpenter, Newfoundland. Dorset bear heads, photograph courtesy Eberhard Otto.*

A Dorset polar bear effigy.

Presumably, this bear carving was the property of a shaman. The neck and chest were hollowed out and in the throat cavity was placed red ochre, probably symbolizing blood. A sliding lid closed this cavity, creating a secret compartment for the ochre. Courtesy Eskimo Realities, *Edmund Carpenter.*

Dorset End Blades.

These tiny stone points were used to tip harpoons.

Chapter IV

Cape Freels

It has recently been discovered that an Indian race of people *were* living side-by-side with the Dorsets for several hundred years in a summer camp at Cape Freels on Newfoundland's northeast coast. Cape Freels, between Bonavista Bay and Hamilton Sound, is one of the richest archaeological sites on the island. In blowing sand-dunes, archaeologist Paul Carignan found traces of ancient campsites.

Charcoal from their fires dated between A.D. 200 and A.D. 750. But who lived there? Paul Carignan could find no trace of the Maritime Archaic at all; no ground slate lances or other tools. But here, as at the Beaches site further south which he also helped excavate, the sea has been nibbling away at the land and slowly flooding it. Maybe the places the Maritime Archaic people lived had been washed away or drowned.

Well then, wouldn't these fireplaces have warmed the chilled hands of the Dorsets who, Dr. Carignan knew, had taken over the coasts two thousand years ago? Except for one or two hide scrapers that may have belonged to the Dorsets, there was no trace of them either.

Unlike those used by the Archaic and Dorset, the arrowheads Paul Carignan kept finding were notched, very much like those of modern Indian tribes. But such an early date! They looked almost exactly like those used by the Beothuk who inhabited the island up to 1829.

Until recently, archaeologists thought the Beothuk had arrived in Newfoundland as recently as 1 000 years ago, about A.D. 1000, about the same time Algonkian peoples moved into Labrador and along the north bank of the St. Lawrence River. It was almost assumed, a few years ago, that the Beothuk were related to these tribes and this migration.

But at Cape Freels, archaeologists, for the first time, found evidence that a relatively modern Indian group lived side by side with the Dorset Eskimos for five hundred years. And they lived there almost a thousand years before any of the other tribes known to the Europeans had come into the area.

What if, on the old shore-line submerged in the sea, were found stone tools which were on their way to becoming notched, as these were, but were old enough to be definitely Maritime Archaic? That would give archaeologists the "hard" proof they needed. As Dr. Tuck had shown in his researches, over the years the stemmed Maritime Archaic stone tools gradually developed a wider and wider base to the stem which would naturally lead to notching. Slender as this proof is, it suggests a distinct possibility that the Beothuk culture developed out of the Maritime Archaic.

Perhaps the missing link has been found. A small site was discovered by Elmer Harp Jr. on the southern shore of Labrador, with dates remarkably close to those tested out at Cape Freels, containing tools that clearly suggest tentative notching.

Donald MacLeod, an expert on the Archaic, believes that "there is still a chance that some Archaic people survived in the *interior* of Newfoundland when the Dorset took over the coasts, and that the Beothuk were their lineal descendants." Prof. James Tuck of Memorial University, who has written a book on Labrador and Newfoundland prehistory, agrees. He says that the Beothuk were, "maybe . . . descendants of the Maritime Archaic people."

The conclusions of the experts in stone tool development are greatly strengthened by a closer look at the Beothuk themselves.

Until very recently, the Beothuk were thought to have had a language unlike any other in the world. Then Dr. Hewson of Memorial University proved that "Beothuk" is a peculiar Algonkian dialect. The Algonkian-speaking peoples include the Montagnais and Naskapi, but also many other tribes, particularly throughout Eastern Canada north of the St. Lawrence, across the northern prairies, and in New England.

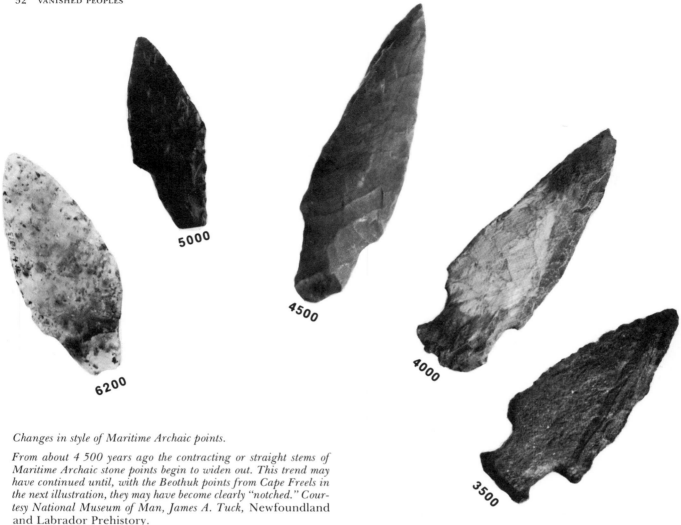

Changes in style of Maritime Archaic points.

From about 4 500 years ago the contracting or straight stems of Maritime Archaic stone points begin to widen out. This trend may have continued until, with the Beothuk points from Cape Freels in the next illustration, they may have become clearly "notched." Courtesy National Museum of Man, James A. Tuck, Newfoundland and Labrador Prehistory.

Probably the Algonkian-speaking peoples (the Algonquin are just one small part of them) are the native group on the continent, most closely related to the Archaic. So, if Beothuk is an *early* Algonkian form, which it well could be, linguistic evidence points to Beothuk descent not from a people like the Montagnais and Naskapi but from the Archaic.

Undoubtedly the most striking evidence lies in the extensive Beothuk use of red ochre. They smeared themselves and all their important utensils with it, and, especially, they used it in their burials. The Archaic made similar use of it — as early as the burial at L'Anse-Amour — *but only the Beothuk of all other peoples in historic times made such extensive use of it.*

The Beothuk lived almost exactly as the Maritime Archaic did, with one important difference. Like the "Shield" Archaic, they relied more heavily than the

Maritime Archaic on caribou. One of the most extraordinary features of the Beothuk that we know about from first-hand accounts is their attempt, every fall, to herd the caribou by means of an incredible network of deer-fences that ran as much as *fifty kilometres* through the bush. These fences were made by cracking tree trunks, about three metres up, and pushing over their tops so that their branches could be tightly interwoven.

Another important piece of evidence shows that they definitely had contact with the Dorset Eskimo. They borrowed from them a distinct variety of that device called the "toggling harpoon head." Made to break free from its shaft, the bone and stone parts of this harpoon head twist inside the animal like a grappling hook. Leverage is exerted by the animal's attempt to escape. As we know, the basic principle for

Stone Beothuk points from Cape Freels.

Beothuk points with the characteristic notching shared by many modern Indian tribes. Courtesy National Museum of Man, James A. Tuck, Newfoundland and Labrador Prehistory.

this device was invented by the Maritime Archaic and borrowed by the early Eskimos. The Dorset refined it and added a separate cutting tip in a slot at its end, which the Beothuk copied.

Imagine then, a highly adaptable people, as the Maritime Archaic were, good at sealing and fishing and using caribou as a back-up resource, suddenly having their coasts invaded by sophisticated Eskimos, highly-skilled in the ways of the Arctic seas, who themselves were being pushed south through Labrador into unfamiliar territory. Unable to match the skill of the Dorsets on the sea they withdrew (copying, in the meantime, their invader's harpoon head). Still visiting the coasts, but not living there throughout the longer and increasingly cold winters, they moved to the interior and began to develop ways to exploit the caribou more efficiently.

According to Shawnadithit, the last of her race, the

Beothuk detested the Eskimos (in her time, those Eskimos who had replaced the Dorset) and called them "Four paws," an insulting epithet suggesting their animality. The Montagnais and Naskapi, who never invaded Beothuk territory, were known as "Shawnamunk", meaning "those friendly ones from the North."

Isolated from contact with the mainland except in very late times, the Beothuk, then, may well have represented the last example of the common Archaic Indian culture. Unlike the Beothuk, the tribes we know today had long before settled into distinct and specialized ways of life. When Columbus and Cabot came searching for the mysterious East, little did they know that, in a way, they had found it. The furthest edge of migration eastwards from central Asia met the leading edge of Western migration, coming the other way out of Europe.

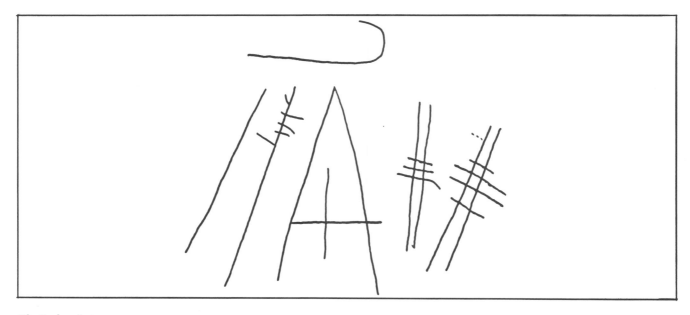

The "ogham" stone.

Less than 16 kilometres away from the Viking site at L'Anse aux Meadows, this strange stone bears an inscription similar to a little-known alphabet called "ogham" used by the early inhabitants of Ireland. *Courtesy* Canadian Geographic Journal.

Chapter V

The Irish and the Norse

Near L'Anse aux Meadows, on a low hill in the bush-land, is a large rock, covered with lichen, on which has been chiselled a message in stone. As yet no one has deciphered it, but it is in a kind of writing that resembles an ancient Irish style called "Ogham", an alphabet that died out in the fifth century and was long forgotten. We might guess, but we shall never surely know, that it was chiselled by St. Brendan the Navigator, the first Irish Christian saint. The Irish legend of St. Brendan tells us that near the end of his life, he set sail with his companions to plant the seed of Christianity in a far Western Isle. The flimsy boat he used, called the currach, was covered with ox-hides. In the summer of 1977 a similar boat was sailed across the Atlantic to Newfoundland just to prove that the feat was possible.

Whoever it was who cut that message in the rock left nothing else behind.

But anthropologist Edmund Carpenter has commented: "Elizabethan England took a belated interest in the New World. To bolster her late claims, she pushed them back. Annalists were set to modifying early manuscripts. Vague Irish and Welsh accounts of distant seafaring were modified to landfalls and settlements along the New England and Carolina coasts. Late 19th century amateur historians used these modified versions, and the damned fakes live on. It's possible the Irish got here, but I agree with Speck: the only reliable evidence is the fact that local Indians were called Micmac."

Blowup of inscriptions from the "ogham" stone. Courtesy Canadian Geographic Journal.

Aerial view of the Norse settlement at L'Anse aux Meadows. Courtesy Parks Canada, Ottawa.

The remains of house E at L'Anse aux Meadows. Courtesy Parks Canada, Ottawa.

In Norse sagas, it is recorded that the boatmen, several times, ran into a group of people they called "Skraelings", in a land across the Western Sea. A great battle ensued with the Norse lucky to escape alive. For years these tales, and others concerning the mysterious Island of Vinland, were thought to hint at a Viking discovery of North America five hundred years before Columbus. Now we know that this was so. On that same tip of Newfoundland, near the Strait of Belle Isle, Professor Ingstad of Norway has recently uncovered the remains of a Norse settlement at L'Anse aux Meadows.

Speculation is that Leif Erikson was the first Norseman to land in Vinland. His father, Eric the Red, had already founded a colony in Greenland which was to prosper for five hundred years and then mysteriously die out. Though otherwise unattractive as a place to live, this rocky point is very strategically located for a seafaring people like the Vikings.

Whether or not L'Anse aux Meadows is the fabled Vinland where Leif the Lucky built his houses is open to question. The earliest of the two Norse sagas, long narrative poems that describe these voyages, were written down a hundred and fifty years after the event, but a reference to Vinland itself was made by a German priest, Adam of Bremen, about the year 1075, almost within living memory of Leif's voyage.

In 1958, Ingstad found a number of grassy humps a half-mile from the present village which reminded him of similar mounds in Greenland and Iceland which had proven to be the remains of sod houses built by early Norse settlers. Later excavations showed these mounds were indeed eight similarly-constructed sod houses with features such as stone lined ember pits where coals were kept overnight to rekindle fires the next morning.

In 1964 a soapstone spindle-whorl used to spin wool was found in one of the mounds, identical to Norse specimens found elsewhere. North American native peoples never used such an object. In 1968, a distinctive bronze pin with a ringed head, made in such a way that it could be clearly dated as belonging to the second half of the tenth century, confirmed that this was indeed a Norse site. Later, remains of a smithy were found, where the Norse had fashioned nodes of iron from a bog nearby. We can imagine the original inhabitants of Newfoundland, attracted by the loud clanging of the hammer on the anvil, watching from their hiding place in amazement at the magic at the forge as the blacksmith pumped his bellows and the charcoal fires roared.

The sagas describe how trading went on between Leif the Lucky, and later Thorfinn Karlsefni, with the "Skraelings". Aware of the superiority of their iron weapons, the Norse refused to trade them for the fur they were offered. Nevertheless some of these weapons were lost in skirmishes with these local inhabitants. And, although Karlsefni's wife, Gudrid, had given birth to a son, Snorri, the settlers decided they could not prosper in this new land, gave up and returned home.

Karlsefni's first encounter with the Skraelings. From the Graenlendinga Saga.

The first winter passed into summer, and then they had their first encounter with Skraelings, when a great number of them came out of the wood one day. The cattle were grazing near by and the bull began to bellow and roar with great vehemence. This terrified the Skraelings and they fled, carrying their packs which contained furs and sables and pelts of all kinds. They made for Karlsefni's houses and tried to get inside, but Karlsefni had the doors barred against them. Neither side could understand the other's language.

Then the Skraelings put down their packs and opened them up and offered their contents, preferably in exchange for weapons; but Karlsefni forbade his men to sell arms. Then he hit on the idea of telling the women to carry milk out to the Skraelings, and when the Skraelings saw the milk they wanted to buy nothing else. And so the outcome of their trading expedition was that the Skraelings carried their purchases away in their bellies, and left their packs and furs with Karlsefni and his men.

Norse artifacts.

Found by Helge Ingstad, these objects confirm a Norse occupation near L'Anse aux Meadows about a thousand years ago. They include a stone lamp, a broken bone needle or pin and a soapstone whorl used on a spindle. The brass pin with the ringed head was distinctively Norse. The container is made of birchbark and may have been used as a fishing float. Courtesy Canadian Geographic Journal.

Side and top views of a metre long plank believed to have been part of a Norse ship. Courtesy Parks Canada, Ottawa.

The geographical description of the Vinland site, of a lake with a short river to the sea up which the Norse could pull their boats, does not correspond with the site in Newfoundland. Nor does the description of the frost-free winters with forage for their sheep and cattle growing all year round. True, the explorations occurred during a warm period, and Leif may have been lucky enough to spend an unusually warm winter, but certainly no wine-grapes could ever have grown in Newfoundland as the sagas describe. On the other hand there were salmon in abundance, good hunting, and good timber — all made much of in the sagas. Furthermore, these explorers from Greenland may not have had a clear idea of what grapes were. "Wine-berries" may have referred to the carpets of blueberries found so abundantly on the peninsula.

Many believe the Skraelings were the last of the Dorset Eskimo, because the sagas describe them as attacking in skin boats. Perhaps they were even the Beothuk, although the description does not fit them so well.

Doubtless the controversy will go on for some time. But does it really matter?

However, the Beothuk did seem to have contact with the Norse. One of the striking things about them, when discovered by Cabot and others, was their extraordinary ability to fashion iron, a trade it seems they could only have learned from the Norse. They must have kept the tradition alive until new sources of iron became available with the second wave of Western Europeans. A surprised Verrazano, in 1523, reported that, unlike the other tribes he had encountered further south, the Beothuk "had learned the use of iron, so in their exchanges with us demanded knives and weapons of *steel*."

The northern tip of Newfoundland.

Labrador is approximately 15 kilometres away across the Strait of Belle Isle.

Chapter VI

Beothuk Life

The variety of the Beothuk's environment was reflected in their way of life. Semi-nomadic, they roamed, like the Maritime Archaic, from the interior to the coast and back again in a yearly round of about 500 kilometres. G.C. Pulling, making inquiries concerning the Indians reported:

They begin coming down the Main Brook the beginning of May & continue passing 'till the 20th. . . . They return to their winter's quarters from about the 1st to the 20th of September, laden with Birds, Eggs, etc. together with what they pilfer from the English. They go several canoes down the Brook, but they are not often seen by Millar's servants. Millar himself said, that some few years ago, he was standing near his own house, four canoes full of Indians stopped opposite to him, and he halloo'd to them. Millar was at this time, at home by himself, which, he says, the Indians knew; for, says he, "The Indians get upon some rising ground in the woods, and watch all our motions." The Indians stopped a few minutes, and then paddled away.

Champlain never saw Beothuk deerfences, but he had his illustrator draw this imaginary version of Hurons driving deer into an arrow-shaped pound as he had described the scene in his Voyages *of 1619. Courtesy James P. Howley,* The Beothuks or Red Indians.

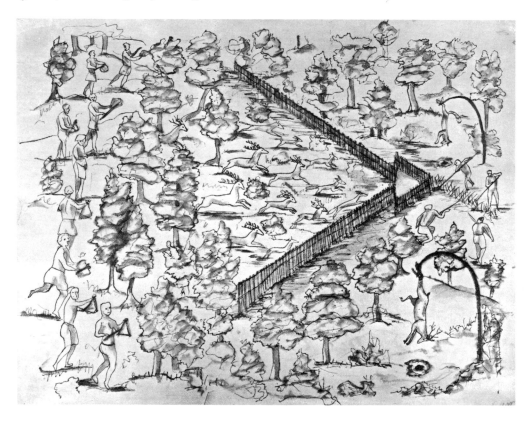

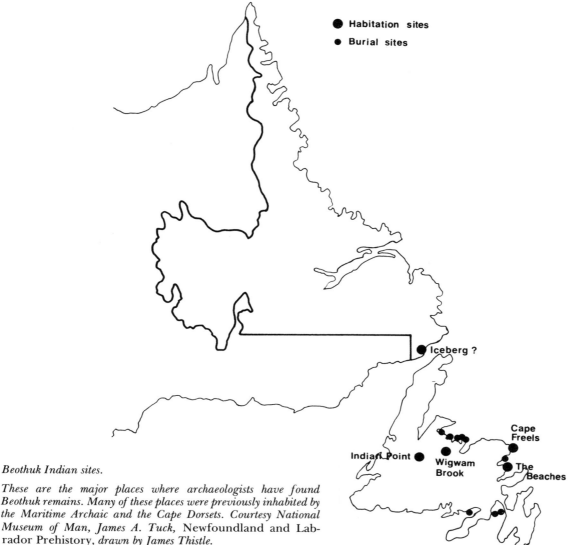

● Habitation sites
● Burial sites

Iceberg ?

Cape
Freels

Indian Point

Wigwam
Brook

The
Beaches

Beothuk Indian sites.

These are the major places where archaeologists have found Beothuk remains. Many of these places were previously inhabited by the Maritime Archaic and the Cape Dorsets. Courtesy National Museum of Man, James A. Tuck, Newfoundland and Labrador Prehistory, *drawn by James Thistle.*

Like many of the Eastern Woodlands peoples, their social organization was loosely knit and centred on small family groups of twenty to thirty people. These were as many as the harsh land would support between the caribou and seal hunting seasons. They had no chiefs, only informal leaders. Probably the Shamans, who conducted ceremonies to appease the spirits of the animals they hunted, were the most influential members of the group.

This informal society paralleled the habits of the Newfoundland caribou, and for similar reasons. In fact, one of the two times a year large numbers of Beothuk congregated was the annual caribou hunt in the fall. Extensive deerfences, sometimes fifty kilometres long, were constructed and maintained by the

A drawing of Shawnadithit annotated by William Cormack.

The "Dancing Woman" is probably wearing a special ceremonial garment. Archaeologist Helen Devereux suspects its fringing is made of bone pendants, many hundreds of which have been found. They may have remained after the leather garments they once decorated deteriorated. The sealing harpoon and the deer spear below are extremely interesting to archaeologists. The breakaway, toggling harpoon point is tipped with an iron endblade and is almost exactly like the Dorset which was tipped with stone. The blade of the deer spear is also iron and is fashioned very much like an old English one. The Beothuk fascination with birchbark can be seen in the way they used it extensively for all their containers and for wrapping provisions, as Shawnadithit has shown here. Courtesy James P. Howley, The Beothuks or Red Indians.

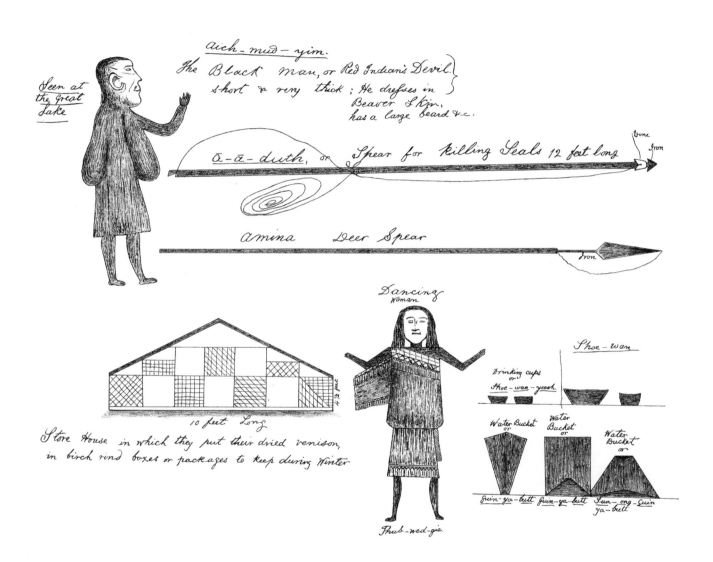

Seen at the Great Lake

Aich-mud-yim.
The Black man, or Red Indian's Devil.
short & very thick; He dresses in
Beaver Skin,
has a large beard &c.

ā-ā-duth, or Spear for killing Seals 12 feet long
bone
Iron

amina Deer Spear
Iron

10 feet Long

Store House in which they put their dried venison, in birch rind boxes or packages to keep during Winter

Dancing Woman

Thub-wed-gie.

Shoe-wan

Drinking cups or Shoe-wan-yeesh

Water Bucket or
Water Bucket or
Water Bucket or

Guin-ya-butt Guin-ya-butt Gun-ong-Guin-ya-butt

group to channel the caribou migration. According to first-hand observers, the trunks of larger trees were cut half through three metres high, and the tree-tops were then pushed down to fall so that their branches could be tightly interwoven. Where trees were scarce, poles were erected and tied with strips of birchbark — or later cloth — to form "sewells" which would flap in the wind. This scarecrow effect kept the herds following natural courses like riverbanks. At the end of the fences, the caribou, pressed together, antlers clacking in panic, would be shot with arrows, speared from raised platforms, or driven into lake waters.

Caribou carcasses were dressed to last the winter. "The manner in which these people preserve their venison is, by taking out the Bones and pressing the Flesh together in squares of four to five feet, and then exposing it to the Frost. We saw 40 to 50 of these square packages." So says an observer in 1781. The packages were stored in provision huts near their encampments. The skins were scraped throughly so that no meat particles, sinew or membrane would remain on the underside to cause the leather to deteriorate. Stone scraping tools ranged in size from large, rough-work types to some small as a fingernail for delicate finishing.

What the Beothuks did to the bones they removed from the meat remains a mystery. Although caribou bones are to be found at these butchering sites, there are also extensive "middens", or garbage dumps, filled entirely with finely-powdered bone. Did these middens have religious significance, or do they merely contain the remains of bones pounded to extract the marrow for food? Described as a neat and tidy people, the Beothuk may have collected and buried this debris rather than let it lie around the camp.

Most of their clothing was made from caribou-hides trimmed with pelts from marten or sable. Men and women alike wore a sleeveless garment like a poncho sewn up at the sides but much longer. They would tie it up around the waist in thick folds, "gird up their loins" when there was a need to act quickly. It could be slipped off the shoulders to draw a bow or throw a spear.

The writer of the Liverpool Manuscript tells us:

On some of their deer skins they draw the figures of men and women, fish, etc. They use awls instead of needles, which they make with fish hooks that they steal. All their cloathing is made of deer skin with the hair on the inside. . . . They sew all their fine work with the tendons of the deer and their coarse work with tough fibrous roots. . . .

Shawnadithit's coat.

This is the back view of a caribou skin coat. Whether it was Shawnadithit's we cannot be entirely sure. It looks very much like a Naskapi coat and may have been given to her. Courtesy Newfoundland Museum.

The "dancing woman" in Shawnadithit's drawing wears a decorated dress with sleeves. It may be a special ceremonial garment or simply come from a later period than those recorded by early observers. "Shawnadithit's coat," which is on exhibition in the Newfoundland Museum, is stencilled and painted like a Naskapi coat. It may have been given to her. Also, the coat was presented to the museum only in the 1940's.

Beothuk grave goods.

A young boy's mocassins and an assortment of beads. Courtesy Newfoundland Museum.

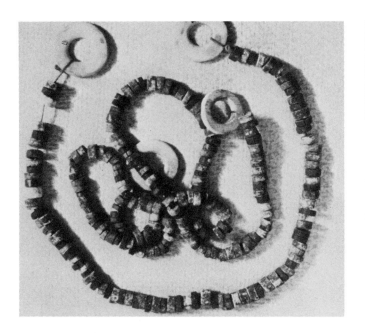

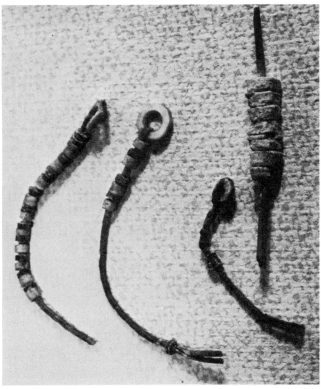

The material most used by the Beothuk besides caribou skins was birchbark. Nearly everything except their clothes was made of it: all their household containers, the linings for storage pits, canoes, summer and winter house-coverings and even their burial shrouds. The pale silver skin of this tree must have had deep significance for them.

Wintering deep in the harsh interior, around the shores of Newfoundland's beautiful lakes, the Beothuk would build their conical birch houses called mamateeks. No other Indian tribe built houses quite like them. Although its roof was shaped like that of a Plains Indian's teepee, the winter mamateek was a permanent structure with a foundation wall. However, unlike the permanent Iroqois longhouses shaped like quonset huts, mamateeks did not shelter a large number of extended familes but only one or two, twelve to thirty people.

Archaeologist Helen Devereux found the foundations of these dwellings at Red Indian Lake, among other places.

It's fascinating to consider how naturally these houses could have evolved. The heart of them was a raised central fireplace. Imagine a campfire throwing its circle of light in the evening. People prepare to sleep close by it by scraping shallow hollows in the sandy soil. Piling the earth on the side away from the fire, they prepare their beds with spruce boughs and fur robes. In the morning, cooking over the heat of the fire, they sit in a circle on the mounds of soil from the sleeping hollows while they chatter and feast. Already we have the basic foundation of the mamateek: the central fireplace, the sleeping hollows around it, the low earth walls to sit on. When the snow falls, all that's needed to complete the shelter is a conical roof with a hole in it to let out smoke and sparks.

Of course these dwellings were not constructed so haphazardly. In fact they were fashioned in a masterly manner, ideally suited for the bitter winters. The low earth walls were wide enough for storage and for extra sleeping hollows. They were not completely circular but six or eight sided. No draft could penetrate.

On top of the walls was erected the four-metre high roof. It was built of raised poles, rather like those in a wigwam, and sheathed, of course, with sewn birchbark. A second layer of poles held this birchbark securely. In turn this layer was sheathed with birch or, in later times, with a stolen sail. The hollow between the two layers of birchbark was stuffed with dried moss to insulate the structure from the cold. Smoke from the hearth escaped through a hole at the top which was lined with clay to prevent fire from flying sparks.

I spent some time dozing in the sleeping hollows found at Red Indian Lake and found them quite comfortable. A mamateek must have been a cozy place as the snow fell outside on its silver skin, flakes hissing round the smoke-hole. In the morning the sun would shaft down into the warm interior lighting up waking faces of children and parents cuddled together under their sleeprobes. There were no cupboards to hide things in. The walls were neatly hung with implements ready at hand and spare materials were stored on beams across the roof away from the inquisitive hands of children.

Beothuk housepit.

Sketch from archaeologist Helen Devereux's field notes of a Beothuk housepit excavation at Red Indian Point on Red Indian Lake. The raised central hearth is surrounded by sleeping hollows. In the foreground is the entranceway. Courtesy Helen Devereux.

Shawnadithit's drawing of a winter mamateek.

Shawnadithit has here attempted to show Cormack the mamateek's basic structure rather than what it looked like when complete, as she knew he had seen several. It is six or eight-sided and is built with a conical roof supported on low walls. The smaller version to the right of the winter mamateek is probably the temporary summer variety which had no foundation walls. The other structure is a square provision shed for preserving pressed squares of caribou meat. Lying about are bits of seal carcass. Courtesy James P. Howley, The Beothucks or Red Indians.

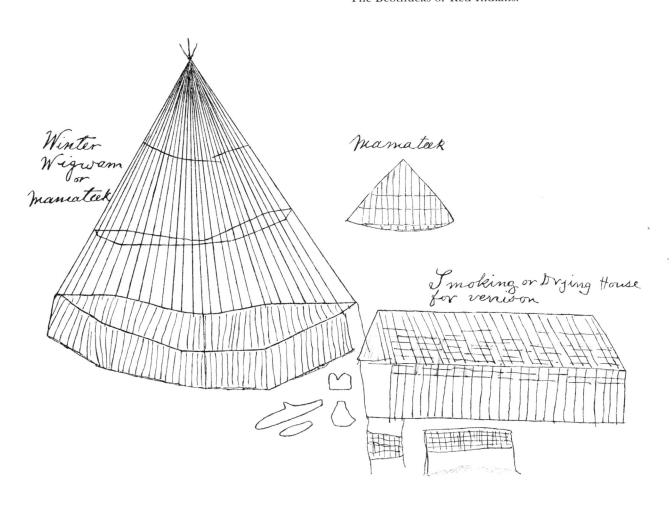

Summer mamateeks were more temporary. They were often described by white settlers since they were found near the coasts. These had no foundation walls. G. C. Pulling comments:

The wigwams are made of a conical form, and look at a distance like a stand of Hop Poles. They are covered with sails if the Indians have any; if not, birch or fir rind is substituted. The fire place is in the centre, and round it are holes dug in the ground, one for each person, where they sit, sleep, and in short remain so long as they are within, for they have but very little room to move about in their wigwams. . . .

Birch was also the material of Beothuk canoes. Its double-bracket shape is unlike that of any other Indian canoe except perhaps the Micmac. This craft is known to us only through tiny models found with burial goods, and descriptions by early observers.

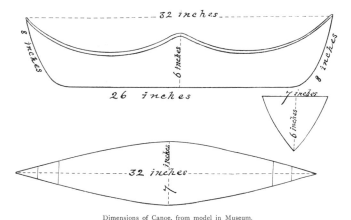

Dimensions of Canoe, from model in Museum.

Joseph Banks, the botanist who joined Captain Cook's expedition to explore the Gulf of St. Lawrence just a few years prior to Wolfe's capture of Québec, came to possess one through a Newfoundland acquaintance who knew he badly wanted to study it. It was sent on Captain Cook's ship to England but was lost when the ship was wrecked in a storm in the Thames Estuary. Although Banks put out notices and offered rewards for its recovery, it has never been found.

Shape of a Beothuk canoe.

No fullscale example of a Beothuk canoe is known to exist. It was shaped very distinctively with high-raised thwarts amidships. Small models of it left in gravesites are in the Newfoundland Museum. Courtesy James P. Howley, The Beothuks or Red Indians.

Although no Beothuk canoe is left for us to try out, contemporary accounts say they were extremely tippy because the hull was not rounded where it met the water. What these early observers did not realize was that Beothuk canoes were ballasted with boulders to make them sit deeper in the water. Portaging simply involved tipping the stones out, then putting new ones in.

The largest canoes, used on large lakes and out in the open sea, were over seven metres in length but weighed only fifty kilograms. Stone ballast was covered over with skins and moss for comfort. The "straight" sides created, in effect, a keel, so that a canoe could be sailed as well. The blades of their paddles were greatly extended so they could be used to punt as well as paddle. Anyone who has tried to wrestle a canoe offshore against a heavy surf will appreciate how useful such a paddle-pole can be.

Contemporary accounts exaggerate the size of these canoes but give due respect to their sea worthiness and Beothuk seamanship.

M'Donald said that he and four other men were on the Funk Island to get Birds, Eggs, etc.; from whence they saw two Canoes, each rowing twenty four paddles on a side, and containing upwards of a 100 of the native savages of Newfoundland. (An exaggeration, the maximum seems to have been twenty.) When they came within Musket Shot M'Donald fired his Piece, loaded with Mould Shot at one of the Canoes. He believes that wounded some of them; but they did not retreat 'till after a second fire. They then paddled off, and went to two small Islands or Rocks, called Gannet Rocks. These are about half a mile to the Northward of Funk Island. Here they landed & took what Birds & Eggs they could find, and then rowed towards Wadham's Island. (The Liverpool Manuscript)

A smaller version of this canoe was thought to be a "fold-up" model. Since it was constructed rather like an envelope with two identical sides neatly sewn at the bottom and covered with resin, a stick holding the raised thwarts apart could be removed and the craft folded flat under the arm for easy portaging. The courses of Newfoundland's inland lakes and rivers are cross-hatched by gravel-bars and other debris left behind by the retreating glaciers. A "fold-up" would make portaging much easier.

The red ochre "ghost" of a large Beothuk canoe was found close to remains of mamateeks by archaeologist Helen Devereux in 1970 on the shore of Red Indian Lake. Although the birch had completely rotted away, the red ochre with which it was smeared stayed as a stain in the sand that had silted over it. Every year this ghostly trace grows fainter and fainter as rain and sun bleach it away. This could well have been the very canoe the explorer James Cormack was to see, beached and silting up with sand, during his melancholy visit to the then deserted area in 1828.

The ravages of white men's diseases, such as tuberculosis, had their worst effects during the long winters the Beothuk spent in the interior. Towards the end of winter, when the food protein needed to fight chronic infections became scarce, many of the old and sick succumbed despite the People's attempt to cure their cough spasms by placing them in steam huts. Like other native peoples, the Beothuks had no natural resistance to tuberculosis and no effective remedies. Demasduit who was captured in 1818 died of this disease as did her child who was left behind. Shawnadithit, the last Beothuk, also fell victim to the "cough demon". There's no doubt this dreadful disease was greatly responsible for much of the Beothuk population decline but it was aggravated by the near starvation they had to suffer from being constantly harassed by the whites from the Twillingate area.

There were many burial practices used by the Beothuk, rather than one, like most other peoples. Again, the various environments they lived in were decisive, not firmly established religious ritual.

If the ground was frozen, the person would be buried in a box-like grave or on a raised scaffold. Otherwise the body would be buried in a stone-covered mound surrounded with personal articles. In all cases, however, birchbark was used to wrap the body, and red ochre was smeared on the body and on all the objects buried with it. Red Ochre and silver birch: blood and skin.

On the coast, burial was usually in natural rock shelters with personal objects, and again red ochre and birchbark.

One site contained a young boy dressed in an entire hide suit, placed close to an adult who may have been his father. Buried with this man was an iron knife and his personal possessions.

Because the soil of Newfoundland is very acid, the only two complete adult Beothuk skeletons in existence were found in rock shelters. They are today in the Newfoundland Museum. Unfortunately, most of these coastal burial places were found by local fishermen; the artifacts have disappeared, and many skulls have been taken for souvenirs. Two such skulls, recently studied by Prof. Devereux, were placed in the Edinburgh Museum. From a note attached, it seems that James Cormack had sent them to a professor working there nearly a hundred and fifty years ago.

A Beothuk doll.

This wooden image was found in a young boy's rockshelter burial. Courtesy Newfoundland Museum.

I.

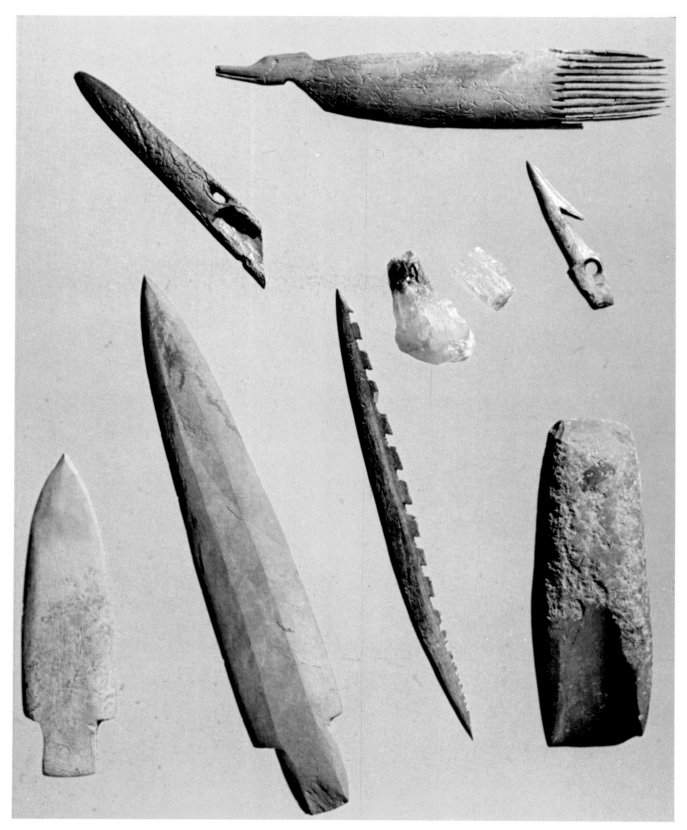

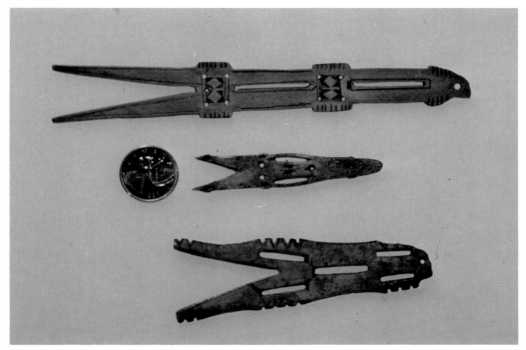

III.

IV.

V.

Domestic articles from rockshelter burials found in the late 19th century. The small birchbark vessels were probably made especially for the ceremony. The wooden bowl may not be of Beothuk origin. Courtesy Newfoundland Museum.

Nearly all the burials and dwelling sites of the
Beothuk contained unique flat bone objects. They
are thin brown slabs of carefully-incised bone, about
fifteen centimetres long and three centimetres wide,
in either a diamond, scimitar or swallow-tailed shape
with a hole at one end. The hole suggests that they
were used as pendants, or, as archaeologist Helen
Devereux speculates, were sewn as fringing along the
bottom of ceremonial garments. The garments rotted
in Newfounndland's acid soil leaving the pendants
behind.

These bone pendants are incised with similar designs, but not one of the many hundreds discovered
are exactly alike. Could these designs have had some
mystical or legend-telling significance? Are they
lineage tables of some sort? We shall never know. If
Shawnadithit explained what they were to James
Cormack, the record is now lost. The archaeologist
Edmund Carpenter, interestingly enough, comments: "Flat stylized bear effigies made by late Dorset
carvers closely resemble 'geometric' carvings made by
the Beothuk." He goes on to say that some of the few
words recorded in the Beothuk language resemble
"special, mysterious and presumably ancient terms
used until recently by East Greenland shamans."
Could these be Dorset words?

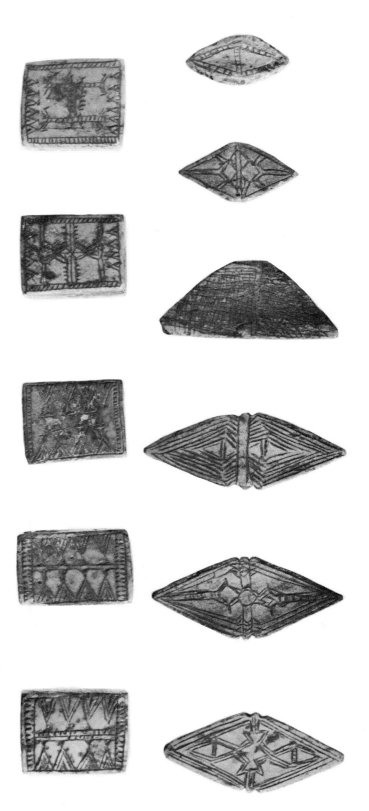

*Beothuk carved ivory and bone pieces, perhaps amulets or gaming
pieces. They probably come from burials but their source is not
definitely known. Courtesy Newfoundland Museum.*

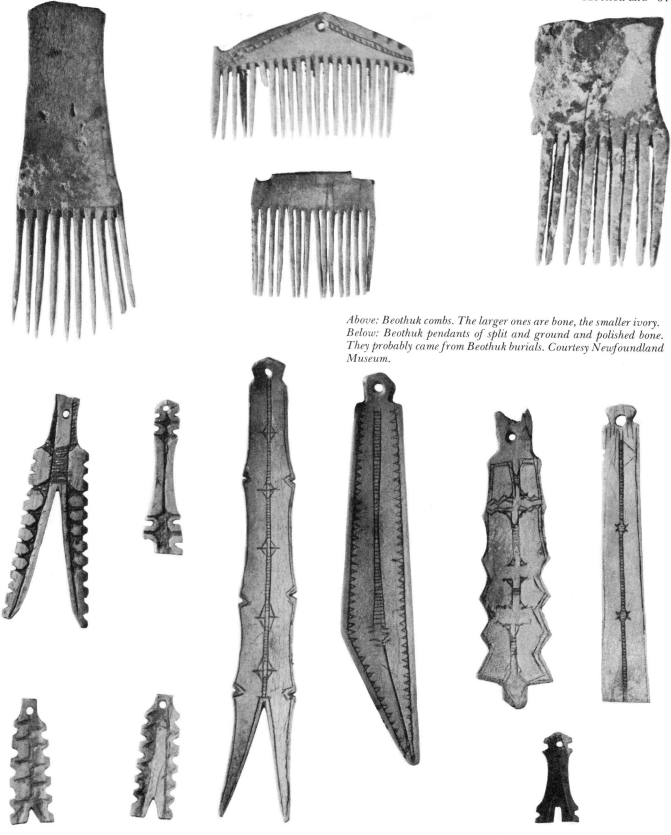

Above: Beothuk combs. The larger ones are bone, the smaller ivory. Below: Beothuk pendants of split and ground and polished bone. They probably came from Beothuk burials. Courtesy Newfoundland Museum.

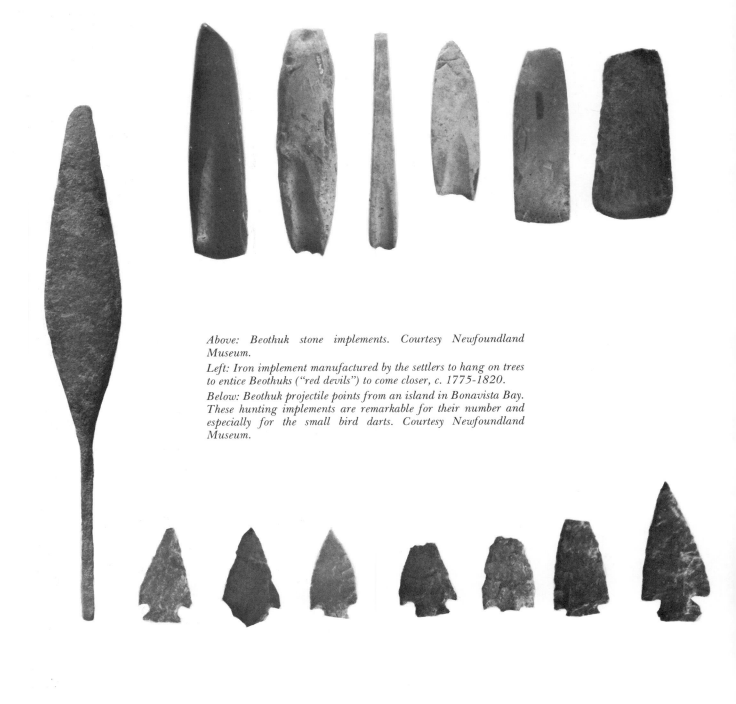

Above: Beothuk stone implements. Courtesy Newfoundland Museum.

Left: Iron implement manufactured by the settlers to hang on trees to entice Beothuks ("red devils") to come closer, c. 1775-1820.

Below: Beothuk projectile points from an island in Bonavista Bay. These hunting implements are remarkable for their number and especially for the small bird darts. Courtesy Newfoundland Museum.

Once spring came, the Beothuk would push off in their canoes to go down the rivers to the coast, taking little equipment since most of it could be fashioned as they went. Stone toolmakers could produce a good arrowhead in about three minutes, using an antler point to put the final fine sharp chips along its edges. Birch vessels were readily made and easily disposable. Water was boiled by throwing red-hot stones into the birch containers so they would not burn. Only the canoes themselves and two hemispheres of iron pyrites were a necessity. These were needed to start a fire. According to one observer, the Beothuk used the breast-feathers of a bluejay as tinder. Returning to traditional campsites on the coasts such as the Beaches, where the animals tended to congregate, they would hunt together again. Did they know the large stone tools they trod on when the tide was low had been made by their ancestors thousands of years before?

The canoes gathered, became a fleet, roaming the island-dotted bays. They hunted seal and walrus not as they are hunted today, during the calving season for the pups' skins, but for meat. They would harpoon them from their canoes in open water.

Shawnadithit, in one of her sketches, drew for James Cormack pieces of seal's fat still on the skin, a bladder filled with oil, and a stomach filled with other seal parts. A knapsack was made of one half of a skin, and a sledge out of one whole one. Other foodstuffs in the same sketch include lobster-tails dried like onions on strings and dried salmon steaks.

Beothuk Iron Implements.

Except for the chisel second from left, all these tools were found at Red Indian Lake. The gouge at left is made exactly like traditional stone gouges. The spear-point is the same style as that represented in Shawnadithit's drawing, and is very like an old English design. To its right is an arrow or dart point. Courtesy Donald MacLeod.

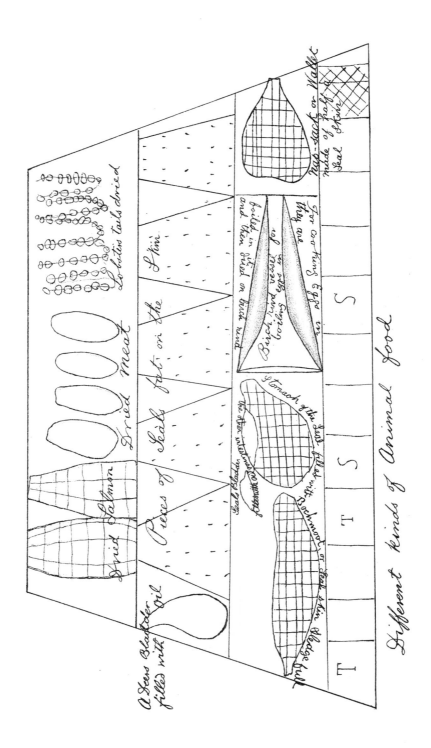

Shawnadithit's drawing of animal food.

From the top left Cormack's notations on this drawing read: "dried salmon, dried meat, lobster tails dried; a deer's bladder filled with oil, pieces of seal's fat on the skin." Upside down is written: "Boch-moot, or seal skin sledge full" and "stomach of the seal filled with the other intestines" (a kind of haggis?). Around the drawings of two birchbark vessels is written, "for cooking eggs in they are boiled in it and then dried on birchrind." Next is a "nap-sack or wallet made of half a seal skin." Courtesy James P. Howley, The Beoth-ucks or Red Indians.

One of a party that had raided a Beothuk mama-teek told the writer of the Liverpool Manuscript:

The only substitute they seem to have for bread is a composition made of eggs mixed with deer's fat & seal's crunceons, and dried in the sun. They generally roast their food, by putting it on sticks, in small pieces round the fire. They boil in birch rind dishes, and keep the water hot, by a succession of heated stones. A flat rock serves them for an anvil to beat out their arrows and spears on. They have frames to spread their skins on to dry. I saw three or four at Indian Cove: These were fastened together with nails they had pilfered from the salmon catchers. . . . The Natives have no Domestic Animals: they drink nothing but water. . . . In the morning, while we were preparing to go away, the young woman combed the child's hair and her own, and then rubbed some sealy fat over it. She then mixed some seal's fat with red ochre and rubbed over the child's body. She pressed us to take more venison; and the old woman got a lump of Deer's fat, melted down very cleanly, and gave it to Thos. Taylor. . . .

Salmon runs were plentiful until the coming of Western Europeans. Not understanding the salmon's life-cycle, the settlers put weirs across the rivermouths to trap them, or strung gill nets. This effectively cut down the number of salmon who could get upstream. The Beothuk ran into trouble by raiding these weirs for fish and stealing the occasional net. G. C. Pulling comments:

Richard Richmond was robbed of his traps up the Rattling Brook last winter. He went in pursuit of the Indians, but could not find them. I told Richmond that I imagined there must have been murder committed on one side or the other, if he had come up with the natives. He said, "Yes, there certainly must, for I should have fired in my own defence, or they would have killed me." — This same man had a fleet of salmon nets taken by the Indians this summer.

The Beothuk paid dearly for their raids, and were sometimes shot on sight, although some settlers allowed their minor pilfering since they realized that the whites were, in effect, stealing the native people's food. The Beothuk fished for salmon themselves, sometimes with stolen nets but most often with a forked fishing spear. But harassment soon drove them into the interior as parties burned their encampments.

Before we left the spot we set fire to three of their wigwams out of four, to be revenged on them for burning a winter-house in the Mouth of the Exploits River. The wigwams we burnt, were covered with sails which the Indians had stolen. We got about 100 deer skins, which we packed up in bundles, one for each man, and made use of seal's skins, by way of sledges to haul them on. In the wigwams we found a Tin Tea-kettle, an Iron Pot, several Traps, & some of our Salmon Nets. The Beds of the traps they had worked into spears & arrows; & some of the nets were picked to pieces to make rope, which they do by platting four parts together. The tea-kettle, pot, traps, etc. with about 500 arrows we threw into the Brook. Thomas Taylor found Rowswell's buckles and some of his button's in one of the wigwams tied up with a piece of fishing line. . . .

Although there was never any trade between the Whites and the Beothuk, we can see from accounts such as these that whitemen's materials were quickly and cleverly adapted to Beothuk needs in their desperate attempt to survive. The fur-hunters' iron traps were specially prized, not for catching small game, but as raw material for fashioning into harpoon and spearpoints, a skill which the Beothuk probably learned first from the Norse. In later days, after they had left the coasts to try living year-round in the interior on sites such as that excavated by Ray LeBlanc near the confluence of the Exploits and Wigwam Brook, the Beothuks' main problems were with the trappers whose gear they were using.

These are thought to be Beothuk carved bone harpoons. The one on the left has a metal end blade bound with sinew. Courtesy Newfoundland Museum.

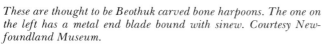

Archaeologist Donald MacLeod digs for shellfish at the spot where the last of the Beothuks probed for mussels to keep from starvation.

The occasional whale seems to have been harpooned, a daring feat from frail birchbark canoes which did not have the ability of Eskimos' kayaks to stay afloat and right themselves when overturned. The small killer-whales which like to feed on salmon close to shore are curious but rarely attack small boats. One of the Maritime Archaic carvings was of a killer whale.

Getting close enough to sink the first harpoon would not be too difficult, but hanging on to the burning line, while your frail canoe was dragged for hours through the water, must have been a terrifying experience.

There was safer fish to be had also: herring, mackerel, cod, and lobster. Shellfish, although not important, were sometimes all that staved off starvation at the end of a long winter before the seal could be hunted safely.

Coast-life lasted about four months, from late May to October, during which time the Beothuk would camp in their summer mamateeks.

On their way back upriver to their ancestral winter homes, the Beothuk would collect berries, hunt small game including beaver, spear salmon in their late runs and club the incredibly tame ptarmigan out of the spruce trees.

Time passed with work on the deerfences, ceremonies, perhaps songs, about which we know nothing except that they were popular. And as the first swirls of snow fell like down, lookouts in tall white pines would scan the fences to announce the return of the godsent caribou.

Reproduction from description of the picture painted for Governor Holloway in 1808, which was to be shown to the Beothuks in the hope of bringing about friendly relations with them. By John Hayward. Courtesy James P. Howley, The Beothuks or Red Indians.

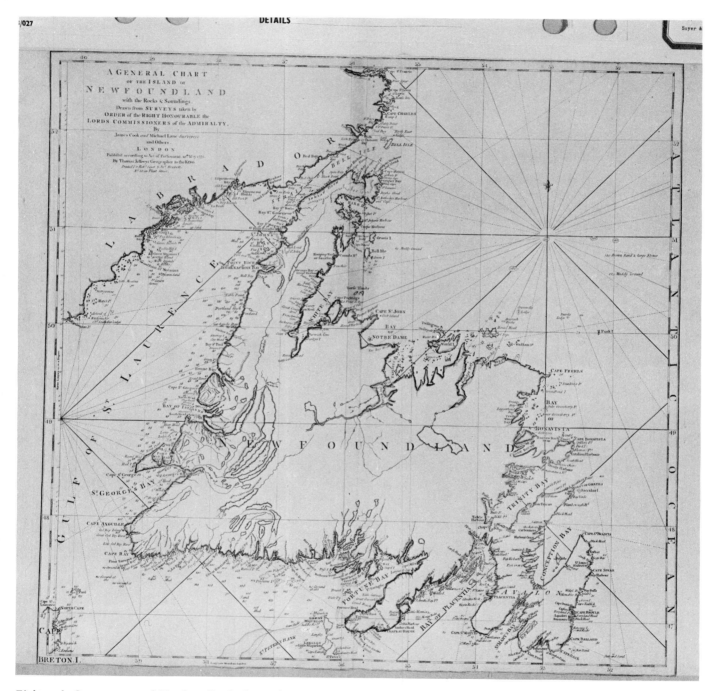

Eighteenth Century map of Newfoundland, drawn by Captain Cook. Courtesy Public Archives of Canada.

Chapter VII

Struggle

The abundant fish resources off Newfoundland had drawn others since the Norse landed at L'Anse aux Meadows.

Confusing as the early reports of Sebastian Cabot's voyages are, it seems probable that on a second voyage one of the Cabots brought back three individuals as curiosities. These people were presented to King Henry VII, according to a contemporary chronicler named Fabian. He notes that:

> Upon two years past after, I saw two apparelled after the manner of Englishmen in Westminster Palace, which at that time I could not discern from Englishmen, till I learned what they were. But as for speech, I heard none of them utter one word.

In 1500 Gasper de Cortereal, with an arrogance characteristic of early explorers, gave the name "Tierra de Cortereal" to the island and Newfoundland appears this way on many early maps. Cortereal also brought back with him, in his two caravels, fifty-seven of the inhabitants.

A letter was written seven days after his landing by Pietro Pasqualigo, Venetian ambassador to Portugal, which concludes coldly:

> They (Cortereal and his crews) have great plenty of salmon, herring, stock-fish, and similar kinds of fish. They have also abundance of timber, and principally of pine, fitted for the masts and yards of ships; on which account his serene majesty anticipates the greatest advantage from this country, both in furnishing timber for his shipping, of which he at present stands in great need, and also from the men who inhabit it, who appear admirably fitted to endure labour, and will probably turn out the best slaves that have been discovered up to this time.

Verrazano in 1523 came back laden with slaves also.

Besides Portuguese slavers, it seems likely, according to J. P. Howley's researches published in 1915, that other Beothuk were carried back by the French. Of one group brought to France in 1608, he quotes Charlevoix's observation: "There is no profit at all to

be obtained from the natives, who are the most intractable of men, and one despairs of taming them."

By this time slaves were a valuable commodity in the European exploitation of the Americas. The Native peoples proved difficult to turn into a labour force for mines and plantations. According to tradition, Christopher Columbus (who was stripped of his governorship and transported back to Spain because of his viciousness) began the slaughter of the Carib Indians. Spanish entrepreneurs continued this extermination and repopulated the Caribbean islands with imported black slaves from Africa. Because many Africans came from semi-feudal systems they were more adaptable, especially since they were torn away from their native lands. Like the Caribs, the Beothuk were an island people who did not have the possibility of moving away from the advancing whites.

The native peoples of mainland Canada acted as prime producers and agents for the Europeans who marketed their catch in Europe. This situation was essentially a co-operative one such as that between the whites and Micmacs in Nova Scotia. The Beothuk, however, were in direct competition with the whites for the fishing resources of Newfoundland's coasts. Because of the whites' superior fishing technology there was never the chance of the Beothuk becoming the prime producers in a co-operative enterprise whereby their catch would be marketed by the whites in Europe.

It is no wonder that the Beothuk, who had the doubtful privilege of being the first inhabitants of North America to encounter Europeans, at first met them with friendliness, then ever after removed themselves from contact as much as they could.

It is only, however, with Jacques Cartier that a clear description of the Beothuk is given, and he made no attempt to exploit them. He arrived in Newfoundland on May 10, 1534, and stayed ten days to provision himself. His stay included a visit for birds and eggs to the Funk Islands, home of the Great Auk, the huge sea-bird that would soon be doomed to extinction by man's depredations.

French explorer Jacques Cartier, 1491–1557. Courtesy Public Archives of Canada.

English explorer Sir Humphrey Gilbert, 1539(?)–1583. Courtesy Public Archives of Canada.

Moving north he put into Quirpon and seems to have met with the Beothuk with whom he traded. Hakluyt, the chronicler, gives Cartier's description thus: "These are men of indifferent good stature and bigness but mild and unruly . . . They are clothed with wild beast's skins . . . They *paint themselves* with certain roan colours. Their boats are made of the bark of birch trees, with which they fish and take great store of seals, and as far as we could understand, since coming hither, that (the Coast) is not their habitation, but they come from the mainland (meaning the interior?)."

Ancient maps always included descriptions of the inhabitants of unknown places, but these are generally unreliable since such passages were often the pure invention of the map-maker.

Sir Humphrey Gilbert and his party took possession of the Island for the Crown of England in 1583. They found no Beothuk at St. John's, but encountered them further north and had friendly intercourse with them. Captain Hoies, second in command, wrote: "In the South ports, we found no inhabitants, which by all likely-hood, have abandoned

these coasts, the same being much frequented by Christians; but in the North are savages altogether harmless." The "Christians" were a mixture of fisherfolk from England, France and Portugal, some of whom may have been wintering over.

Through the seventeenth century other contacts were made by John Guy in 1612, Captain Richard Whitbourne 1622, and Sir David Kirke, 1638. They and others all mention that by this time the Beothuk were not to be seen in the south and east parts where the English had become numerous, but dwelt in the north and west.

In the north and west they came into contact with the French, who still maintained fishing rights there in the uneasy struggle between the French and English for ownership of the island. At first this contact was friendly. Richard Whitbourne mentions that the French and Biscaines "report them to be an ingenious and tractable people (being well used); they are ready to assist them with great labour and patience in killing, cutting and boiling the whales; and making the traine oyle, without expectation of other reward than a little bread or such small hire".

A Fishing Station in Placentia Bay, Newfoundland, *about 1690. Oil painting by Gerard Edema, Sigmund Samuel Canadiana Collection, Royal Ontario Museum, Toronto, Ontario.*

But relations with the French later deteriorated and may have led to armed conflict and the slaughter of small French settlements at St. Julien and Croque in Northern Newfoundland. However Howley, author of the compendium *The Red Indians of Newfoundland,* is of the opinion these were not Beothuk at all but Montagnais or Naskapi from the mainland on a raiding party.

There is another tradition that Guy had arranged to meet the Beothuk the following year at the place where he had first established friendly relations with them. Unfortunately a fisherman preceded him and seeing a large party gathered on shore, fired into them with cannon.

Micmac Indians, *anonymous, possibly by Elizabeth Ladd, painted in the 1820's, National Gallery of Canada.*

Whatever the case, from the middle seventeenth century onwards, the Beothuk were treated as inconveniences to be disposed of and were slaughtered on contact. This situation was compounded by the migration of Micmacs from Nova Scotia into the Western part of the island. Unlike the Beothuk, the Micmacs co-operated with the Newfoundland fur-traders. Equipped with whitemen's boats and fire-arms, they were able to make the crossing more easily than before and also to overcome the Beothuk who had a great fear of guns and never used them.

Another tradition perpetrated by the English settlers, who began to replace the French in the northern parts of the island was that the French had offered a bounty to the Micmac for each Beothuk killed. Howley disputes this idea also, saying that such

a practice "is at variance with the general treatment accorded the native tribes of America by that nation and is hard to believe. The French, it is well known, always held that the Indians were human beings, with souls to be saved, not mere animals to be destroyed." Later Howley asserts, "Once an old Micmac remarked to me, 'Red Injun not bad man, if he mind to he could kill every fisherman without letting himself be seen at all.' " There are no instances of Beothuk ever having attacked a white settlement, or of revenging themselves upon those who did not molest them. The Beothuk, however, were not above practical jokes such as throwing snow down onto men in sawpits, or stuffing large dead geese and setting them afloat to watch the whitemen blast at them with shotguns.

A similar kind of prank served a very practical purpose:

Just as we got into the cove we saw a young water pigeon that had its throat partly stopped to prevent its diving & we supposed.... the Indians had placed it there to know if we had any guns, for if we had they supposed we should fire at it; & as we did not fire, they took it for granted we were unarmed, & conducted themselves accordingly. (The Liverpool Manuscript)

By the end of the seventeenth century, the Beothuk were always called, as Howley's Micmac describes them, "Red Indians" or "Redskins". This was a name that stuck to the other tribes of North America incorrectly, since it derived from the Beothuk habit of covering themselves with red ochre.

But slaughter of the Beothuk by whites was not the only trouble they had to contend with. Perhaps more serious was the disturbance that white settlement made to their delicately balanced relationship with the land on which they lived.

It's an astounding fact that no consistent contact was made between the English and the Beothuk for two hundred years. But all this time, the Beothuk population must have been dwindling as their life became progressively more disrupted and they hid themselves in the wild interior. First, they had difficulty freely visiting the coast and the islands which the fishermen were exploiting. Howley recounts legends that they continued visits to Funk and Fogo Islands in dense fog, presumably navigating across sixty kilometres of open ocean by sensing the currents they could feel against their knees in their frail craft.

A contemporary records that, "It is wonderful how they find their way about in the thickest fogs as they do. They will go to the Funk Island, which is 15 leagues from the Main Land, & return from it in the thickest weather." (*The Liverpool Manuscript*) During fog, the sea would tend to be calmer, but such a journey is almost inconceivable.

Soon most of the rivers were strung with fishing weirs so that much of the salmon run was lost to them. The partridges, which Cartwright in 1768 described as being "almost reckoned as a kind of domestic poultry to the Indians" were greatly reduced in numbers and ultimately the hinterland was trapped by European "furriers" who eliminated the beaver, marten, sable and other small game the Beothuk relied on. Lastly, the caribou, on whom they had become most dependent, began to change their already uncertain migration routes. With a population depleted to less

Major John Cartwright. Courtesy James P. Howley, The Beothuks or Red Indians.

than a few hundred by the mid-eighteenth century the Beothuk could no longer organize the building of deerfences and from then on were reduced to hectic scavenging. Folktales report that the whiteman's dogs were sent to drive them into the open lakes to be shot for Sunday sport, like deer.

Sir Joseph Banks never met the Indians, but was a reliable reporter. He tells of the relations existing between the two groups in his diary of 1766:

Our people, who fish in these parts, (in the neighbourhood of Fogo Island) live in a continual state of warfare with them, firing at them whenever they meet with them, and if they chance to find their houses or wigwams as they call them, plundering them immediately though bows and arrows, and what they call their pudding (made from dried eggs), is generally the whole of their furniture.

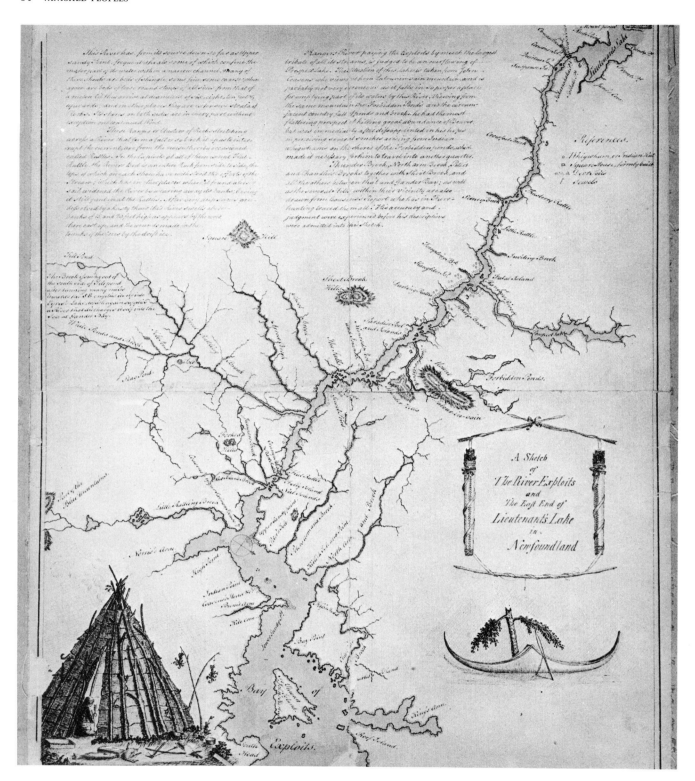

A Sketch of the River Exploits and the East End of Lieutenant's Lake in Newfoundland, 1768, *by Lieutenant* *John Cartwright. Courtesy of the National Map Collection, the Public Archives of Canada.*

Two years later, in 1768, Lieutenant John Cartwright, a sympathetic humanitarian, made a long report to Governor Hugh Palliser detailing the Beothuk way of life as he had seen it in a journey up the Exploits River. He reported several incidents of brutality against the Beothuk. Cartwright was pleased to see the following year that the new Governor, Sir John Byron, immediately issued a proclamation which read in part: "I do also require and command all officers and magistrates to use their utmost diligence to discover and apprehend all persons who may be guilty of murdering any of the said native Indians, in order that such offenders may be sent over to England to be tried for such capital crimes."

Settlement had been discouraged in Newfoundland so that British fishing barons would not be threatened with home-grown competition. In consequence, Newfoundland was settled in the north by many escapees from press-gang service in the British navy and other outcasts from the law. The settlements had no real law and order. The situation was similar to that of the American "wild west". Most of the population was male. In 1774 there were five times as many men as women, and of those few females, 63.5% were servants in upper-class households. Thus true family life was rare.

Justice was carried out on the yardarm principle by whichever ship's captain happened to put in there. "Anyone to hang? Anyone to marry?" was their general attitude. With no real system of justice in the island we can see why Byron's proclamation includes the order that offenders "be sent over to England." John Cartwright's brother, George, made a strong plea for courts to be established in Newfoundland, at an official inquiry at which he gave evidence.

With the authorities awakened to the situation, an investigation was carried out by Magistrate John Bland of Bonavista in 1792 who heard rumours that a series of killings had been perpetrated by John Peyton Sr. of Twillingate, an important fishery owner, and an assorted gang of independent British furriers and fishermen. His report was lost until it was recently discovered by Nimshe Crewe, a Newfoundland archivist in the archives of the first Earl of Liverpool.

Known as "The Liverpool Manuscript", the report contains an official account of the questioning of the principals in these incidents. Thomas Russel (variously spelled Rowsell and Rousell in this and other accounts) was a noted Indian killer who was finally ambushed at his fishing weir and killed by the Beothuk in 1789. Taking this as an excuse, John Peyton

Sr., Thomas Taylor and others went marauding, killing several Beothuk. The manuscript contains their accounts of this expedition and others which, although very evasive, are suggestive of great cruelty.

In another incident recorded in this manuscript Thomas Taylor, Richard Richmond and William Hooper lost some nets and went up to the Beothuk encampment at Charles Brook to look for them. There they saw a punt which the Beothuk had stolen in retaliation for a canoe stolen shortly before by the settlers. Two women ran out of the wigwam and hid. Then a man came out with a little boy under his arm and stared sternly at them. The manuscript goes on:

Richard Richmond desired Thos. Taylor to fire . . . Taylor fired and wounded the man in the thigh and the boy in the heel. The man let the boy fall and was running off when William Hooper . . . fired, and struck him between the shoulders: upon which he immediately fell, and soon expired. All the rest made their escape except the girl (who was in the possession of Mr. Stone, Merchant, near Poole, but is now dead) and the little wounded boy. The former they brought away with them . . . but the latter they left to perish, because they thought he would not recover from his wounds.

In an earlier expedition of 1781 included in the manuscript, the writer mentions Peyton's own account of battering a wounded Indian to death with a trap the Indian had stolen from him.

. . . in one of the wigwams was a man so much wounded as not to be able to stand. — One of Peyton's traps was lying by him, the bed of which he had been beating into arrows on a flat stone which served as an anvil. When they entered the wigwam, the wounded man sat on his bench & defended himself with the remaining part of the trap: but being soon overpowered, Peyton wrested it from him, & beat out his brains with it.

The manuscript was given further credence by the discovery of what appear to be field notes for it written by one G. C. Pulling. This field document differs only slightly from Bland's neater official report. But Bland had no hard evidence to go through the tiresome business of bringing them to justice.

Interestingly, J. P. Howley, who did not know these documents existed, gives a folklore account of the same atrocities which, of course, is even more damning of Peyton and the others than their own account.

In 1790 Bland wrote, "Peyton has rendered himself infamous for his persecution of the Indians. The stories told of this man would shock humanity to re-

A Beothuk vocabulary, assembled by G.C. Pulling in his field notes investigating the relations between settlers and Beothuks in the Twillingate area, 1792. A photocopy of the original is available in the Centre for Newfoundland Studies, Memorial University, St. John's, Newfoundland.

late." And he recommends to the Governor's secretary that Peyton be expelled from the area. Unfortunately the suggestion was never carried out because Peyton and the furriers continued their slaughter and were key figures in the last years of the Beothuk. For example, as Thomas Taylor recounts:

Mr. Peyton, Millar & myself went three day's journey up the Main Brook — on the third morning, at day-break, we saw the tracking *of an Indian. . . I looked, but could see none, for by the time I came up he was gone, but soon after we saw a great number of them in the landwash spreading skins. They ran to their wigwams, and we pushed on. They stood together in a large body, near their wigwams and we thought best to fire. (The Liverpool Manuscript)*

There is a strong tradition in Newfoundland reported by Howley, that, in 1800, three or four hundred of the Beothuk were driven out onto a long point of land near their favourite sealing site and shot down like deer. Although the name is not the official one, present-day inhabitants of the area still call the place "Bloody Reach" and it seems from archaeological investigation that the site was abandoned and never revisited after 1800.

This incident, which like most others is not documented officially, marked the beginning of the end for the Beothuk. From this time, virtually all the maritime activities of their life were closed to them. In the harsh interior, hounded on all sides, they would make their way as best they could. John Bland's prediction in 1790 that "before the lapse of another century, the English nation, like the Spanish, may have affixed to its character the indelible reproach of having extirpated a whole race of people" was to come true much sooner than he predicted.

The Beaches site, Alexander Bay. This arm of the sea is still locally known as "Bloody Reach". It may have been the location of a legendary massacre of several hundred Beothuks.

Back Harbour, Twillingate.

*Twillingate sits on territory formerly occupied by native Newfound-
landers for several thousand years. Courtesy D. MacLeod.*

Chapter VIII

Capture

The threat of punishment in Governor John Byron's proclamation in 1769 did not seem to deter the whites' extermination of the Beothuk. Then, shortly after 1800, a reward was offered for capturing a Beothuk alive. Whites in the nineteenth century assumed that they were the highest form of human life. They looked on Native Peoples as children who needed to be educated for menial work, taught proper manners and introduced to the concepts of Christianity. Even humanitarians like Bland, the Cartwrights and later William Cormack thought it their duty to "civilize" the Indians rather than to help them to survive in their own ways. Once an Indian was captured, they thought he could be treated with extreme kindness, taught the whitemen's ways, and returned to the tribe to act as ambassador between the two warring groups.

Two male Beothuk had been brought up by the whites from early childhood: one called June and the other August (named after the months of their capture). June had died long before. August, who was dropped from his mother's back when she was shot, in 1768, had given no information about Beothuk customs, language or habits since he had been four years old at the time. He died on October 29, 1788.

William Cull, the master of a fishing vessel, was the first to take advantage of the newly-instituted reward, bringing to St. John's a woman he had seized "by surprise" in the neighbourhood of the Bay of Exploits. By now, the Exploits River and Red Indian Lake, from which it flowed deep in the interior, were the only regions the Beothuk were known to inhabit. Cull was given £50 and ordered to return the woman to her tribe with clothes and presents Government House provided. Many people believed that he in fact murdered her and made off with the baubles. His own short letter to the admiral's secretary states that he left her in her countryside and ends:

I would not wish to have any more hand with the Indians unless you will send round and insure payment for a number of men to go into the country in the winter. The people do not hold with civilizing the Indians, as they think they will kill more than they did before.

On July 30, 1807, Governor Holloway increased the reward to £100. There is no doubt that this offer had the opposite effect to that intended. To wrest a member from the tribe would entail violence and perhaps many were slaughtered by such kidnap attempts. It is significant that only women were ever captured by the settlers.

Accounts indicate that women were treated with great respect by the Beothuk and whenever in danger from white men they would kneel and throw open their robes revealing their breasts to indicate their sex. That such gestures were ignored is related over and over again in the accounts. Cartwright gives a particularly gruesome example in his report, of the murder of a pregnant woman. Revealing herself, she had begged for mercy but had been cut into pieces. Boastfully, one of the killers had shown Cartwright her cut-off hands.

The proclamation was reissued by Governor Duckworth in 1810 in the name of King George III. Since nothing came of it, the government decided to mount a quasi-military expedition under Lieutenant John Buchan. Buchan has written us a long account. His report was corroborated in nearly all respects by Shawnadithit when she was questioned by William Cormack in 1829. We have left to us, in fact, a remarkable series of "story maps" and drawings made by her and annotated by Cormack. Taken together, they give us a vivid account of the Beothuk's last days.

Captain David Buchan. Courtesy James P. Howley,
The Beothuk or Red Indians.

Buchan's expedition, begun in early January, 1811, ended tragically because he failed to take into account the character of the men he assembled for his party from the neighbourhood of Twillingate. They were hated fur-trappers and fishermen that the Indians knew by sight. William Cull, for instance, was a guide and the twenty other locals recruited to swell his marine contingent of twenty-one included Thomas Taylor, mentioned as one of the Indian killers in the Liverpool Manuscript.

Close to Beothuk habitation, half the men remained behind with the sledges and the others continued at a faster pace. They surprised the Beothuk at their settlement and held friendly parlay with them in their largest mamateek (close quarters with forty people inside!). James Butler and Tom Bouthland, both marines under Buchan's command and not local inhabitants, volunteered to stay with the Beothuk while repairing their snowshoes, while the rest of the party and four Beothuk went back to the place where the others were guarding the sledges.

That Buchan allowed these two to stay was also a mistake, but his hopes of establishing friendly relations seemed to be going so successfully he thought it would be an extra gesture of trust.

The cache was a long way back, however, and although the four Beothuk appeared cheerful, they must have felt apprehensive accompanied by twelve armed white men and being led away from the security of their camp. Two of them, one being Nonosabasut their last leader, left the party when they came to Buchan's empty fireplace of the night before, but indicated the two others were to stay with Buchan. These two became more suspicious until, near the base-camp, one fled, yelling to his companion to follow. His companion was persuaded to remain with the party, but a little further on became very frightened at the sight of twelve more armed men waiting to greet him.

Shawnadithit, many years later, told Cormack that the man who had fled was her uncle, Lognon. He had seen a campfire and realized more men were waiting — something he hadn't expected. He ran back to his fellows, desperate to warn them that there were enough armed men to wipe them out entirely.

What should they do? Time was short. The whites had seemed friendly enough, had even left two hostages behind. But how could they trust them, when some of the men with Buchan were known murderers of their relatives?

The tribe decided to move from the Lake and conceal themselves deep in the woods. They began gathering their goods, piling them on sleighs, and taking as much food as they could carry. When they were ready to go, the hostages, naturally enough, refused to go with them. Now what were they to do? They couldn't make good time if they had to force-march or carry these two. And if they left them behind, they might be able to track them from a distance and report their whereabouts to Buchan. Lognon urged the tribe to kill them although Shawnadithit said they debated what to do for a long time. They drew lots to see who should have the dishonour of killing the captives, shot them in the back quickly when they were not looking, elected an old woman to cut off their heads in the traditional way and stuck them on two poles. Then they fled.

When Buchan returned this was the sight that greeted him. The remaining Beothuk hostage managed to run away. Shawnadithit reckoned the tribe was only seventy people at this time. She was a girl of eleven.

That the local inhabitants used this incident as an excuse to revenge themselves on the Beothuks and exterminate them seems probable. Another drawing of Shawnadithit's is marked "Showing that the murder of them was going on in 1816."

This drawing is interesting in other ways. Cormack, in his researches, was friendly with John Peyton's son, John Peyton Jr. "Young" Mr. Peyton seemed to be disposed to the Beothuk differently from his father and of a humanitarian cast of mind as was Cormack. Throughout, Cormack seems to protect the reputation of the elder Peyton, not knowing half of what we do now. On this map, which he annotated for Shawnadithit, the words "Mr. Peyton" and "murder" were both originally left out. These words were added later, probably by J. P. Howley in the course of his research. He, too, was friendly with "young" Peyton (by now an old man) who helped him enormously in his researches, even giving him access to his personal diary recounting his, and his father's, dealings with the Beothuk.

Unfortunately, the family destroyed the diary quite recently, fearing for their reputation. Is it possible that during the confusion of printing his compendium, Howley omitted to erase those words he had earlier added? His book took over forty years to compile. Howley's notes to this map, which he printed in his book *The Beothuks*, describe the notation of the drawings the way Cormack had left it, with no reference to added words and with Peyton's name omitted!

Except for Governor Keat's proclamation of 1813, repeating the previous offers for capturing a Beothuk, nothing was done officially to establish contact after this expedition, although Lieut. Buchan requested it. In fact, he may have led an unofficial expedition in 1815 or 1816. Cormack's notes sometimes use 1816 as the date of Buchan's trip, rather than 1811, and "E.S." (probably Edward Slade) mentions this date in his account of the next important contact made with the Beothuk in 1819. This account was published in the *Liverpool Mercury* of late 1829. Slade's account also includes evidence of a man named Rogers from Twillingate who, with three others, murdered nine Beothuk in 1817 and showed Slade the pile of bones on an island a year later.

John Peyton Junior, Justice of the Peace, Twillingate. Courtesy Newfoundland Museum.

They reach this at night and encamp in the woods see off early next morning across the Lake

Reach this before day-light and remaining for day and a half waiting for rendezvous with Capt. B. two encamped with Capt B. and who escaped and joined them here.

Indians crossing the Lake

Island

half a days march across

a small party that were encamped here remove & join the main body of the Tribe

encampment

A

The whole Tribe encamp here and remain (the Winter)

Shawnadithit's story-map of Buchan's expedition in 1810-11.

Although it was drawn for Cormack nearly twenty years after the event (at which time she was ten or eleven), Shawnadithit's story of Buchan's visit from the Beothuk point of view, corroborates his official account almost exactly. Although it is out of scale, the Red Indian Lake area is rendered by her in minutely accurate detail. The Indians are drawn in red.

Cormack's explanation at bottom centre reads:
Marines Head stuck on a pole around which the Indians danced and sang two hours in the woods at A, they having carried the head with them the other marines head they left at B and on their return there in the Spring they danced and sang in like manner.

Marines Head which the India two hours in th having carried the the other marin B and on their Spring they dance in like manner.

Captain Buchan's visit to the Red Indian

First night of retreat reach this Spot 2 have until found by 5 men & 4 women 3 boys and three 4 girls who occupied these two wigwams.

Mary march's cemetary

B

Red Indians retreating

Bank party on the ice to surprise the Indians = ing marines after Kill

Capt Buchan

Killing Marines

the 3 wigwams taken by Capt. B

nancy's uncle running from to Capt. B. after returning from the Lake and interspersing what had happened (trousers thrown away during his flight)

Nancy's Fathers wigwam

Nancy's uncles wigwam

Mary March's Fathers wigwam

Capt. B's party returning for presents with 6 of the Indians

(the 4 Red Indians return from Capt. B here)

One of the two Red Indians desert Capt. B here

Luggage left here by Capta. Buchan untill his return from the great Lake

(42 men with Capt. B — 2 killed)

tuck on a pole arround danced and sang woods at A. they head with them head they left at turn there in the and sang round it

A

by Shannadithit

in 1810–11 when the two marines were killed.

Shawnadithit's story-map of a murder in 1816.

"accompanied with 2 others old . . . killed Woman at A 14 or 15 years ago on the Exploits river" was the way Cormack's notation probably read on this map. Did J. P. Howley add the name Mr. Peyton and forget to erase it before he published this map in his compendium? Courtesy James P. Howley, The Beothucks or Red Indians.

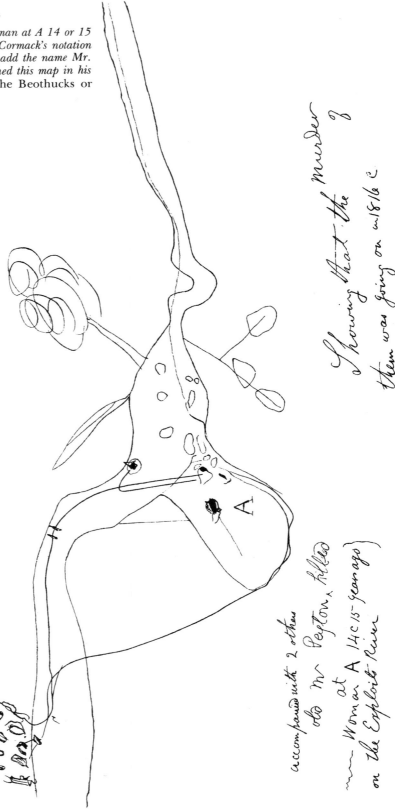

drawn by Shanandithit

Showing that the murder of them was going on in 1816 ?

accompanied with 2 others old Mr Peyton, killed Woman at A 14 c 15 years ago on the Exploits River

Red Indian Point.

The main Beothuk village on Red Indian Lake.

In 1818, the Beothuk, desperate for provisions, cut adrift a boat of John Peyton's containing salmon for St. John's, while his crew were asleep on shore waiting for the tide to turn. Beaching it, they took a waistcoat containing Peyton's watch and some other articles from its cuddies. Firearms found on board were mangled and flung into a creek.

Waiting until wintertime, Peyton the younger got permission to go up the Exploits River with the dual purpose of recovering his personal property (which included some money) and of attempting to capture a Beothuk for the reward.

There are many accounts official and unofficial of this trip, but the main facts are clear. They surprised the Beothuk by travelling without fires on the river and lake ice in March of 1919. Their gun-shots set the Beothuk running across deep snow on the lake. The small terrified band picked up their children and ran into the woods. One of them, Nonosabasut, to whom everyone looked for leadership, had been given his precious child by his wife Demasduit. In the safety of the woods, he turned in time to see Demasduit stumble and fall on the snow of the lake. Before he could find someone to hold their baby and get back to help her, she was overtaken by John Peyton. In the traditional gesture of begging for mercy, Demasduit opened her garment to show she was a woman and Peyton's party surrounded her, gleeful at the thought of taking home a captive and sharing the reward.

Shawnadithit's map showing Buchan's visit and the taking of "Mary March" (Demasduit).

These two incidents were central to the fate of the Beothuk. It is natural for Shawnadithit to illustrate them together on the same map. Courtesy James P. Howley, The Beothucks or Red Indians.

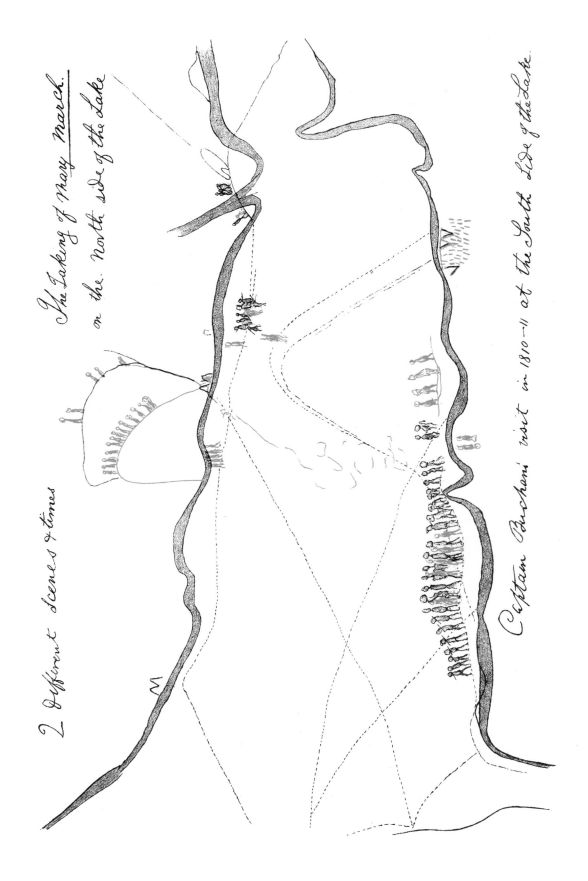

2 different scenes & times

The taking of Mary March.
on the north side of the Lake

Captain Buchan's visit in 1810–11 at the South side of the Lake.

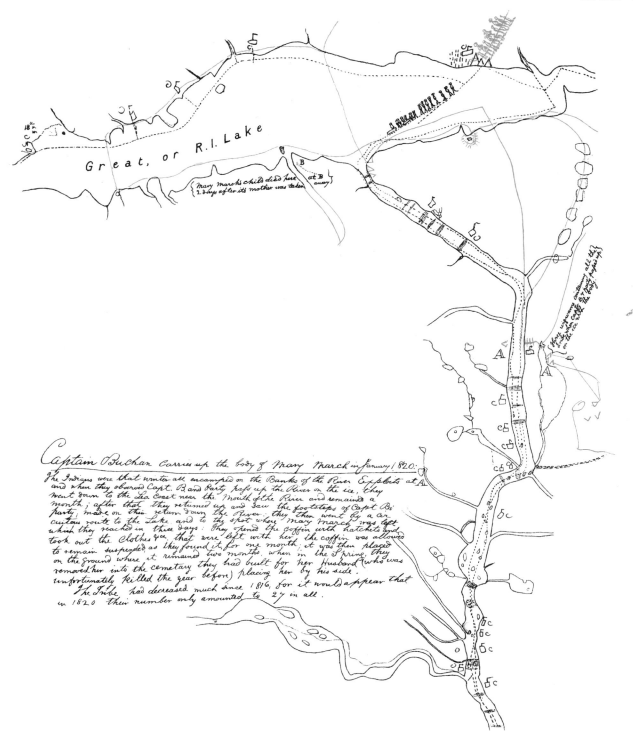

Shawnadithit's map describing the return of Demasduit.

It appears from this map that only three wigwams containing all the survivors of the tribe were left. They were encamped on the East side of the River Exploits, just below where it ran from Red Indian Lake. The Indians saw Buchan pass with his men carrying the pine coffin which they left by the sepulchre where the Indians had buried Demasduit's husband. *Courtesy James P. Howley,* The Beothucks or Red Indians.

Demasduit, or "Mary March". Portrait by Helen S. Parsons, 1951. Courtesy Newfoundland Museum.

The people were yelling, "Demasduit! They've captured Demasduit." Nonosabasut ran back onto the open lake towards Peyton's party. Any minute they could open fire and shoot him down. He kept going. Two of his bravest friends had joined him on either side. They slowed to a walk. Maybe the invaders were keeping Demasduit as a hostage because they thought there were more Beothuk than there seemed.

Now they were standing there with their guns ready, pointed. They kept walking. Demasduit was struggling and shouting Nonosabasut's name. "Don't worry Demasduit. The baby's safe. Don't worry."

The invaders waved to him to come forward by himself and drop his weapons. They didn't know he still had an axe under his garment. They gestured to his friends to stay back. So they wanted to talk. One of his friends brought him a spruce bough, the emblem of peace and friendship. Nonosabasut came forward waving it.

Peyton's party watched him come close. He was a huge fellow towering over them all. Maybe if they captured him too they'd get twice the reward. With gestures he let them know he wanted the woman to be released. Peyton shook his head. "No, she's going with us. You can come too if you like." The tall Beothuk began waving the branch and made a long speech. Then he threw the branch down, his face flaring with anger. He made a grab for Demasduit. They struggled with him and he drew back. Then he took out the axe.

Before he could use it, one of the men stabbed him in the back. He whirled, grabbed the dagger and went for Peyton. Edward Slade grabbed at his arm but he flung him off and turned to fight the others. Someone fired a shot into his belly. The attackers stood back. But he wasn't dead. He looked dizzily around at them still restraining Demasduit. Then he saw the man who had first stabbed him. With a wild yell, he rushed at him. But the man fired and Nonosabasut collapsed dead onto the bloody snow in front of his wife. According to Slade, one of the men measured Nonosabasut as he lay, finding him to be over "six feet seven inches."

Demasduit, called Mary March, was taken to St. John's, exhibited there, then ordered by the Governor to be returned by Lieutenant Buchan. In the meanwhile the young child she had left behind had died. Buchan took her back to Twillingate but she died from tuberculosis on board his ship before contact with her people was made. Buchan took her body in a pine casket up to the Lake in winter where he discovered a sepulchre raised to house Nonosabasut and their child. He left Demasduit there and, according to Shawnadithit, the People placed her beside her husband. This sepulchre was found by Cormack on his melancholy expedition to the Lake in 1826. It has since been lost forever because a logging dam which has raised the water-level some ten metres since the 1880's.

According to Cormack's notes on Sketch 3, the tribe was reduced, by 1820, to only twenty-seven people, a frightened, probably inbred, tiny band of scavengers, virtually captives confined to their ancestral lake. Only these were left to carry the memory of a once prosperous people.

Shawnadithit's story-map of the Beothuk's last encampment.

Here are all the sorry details of the tribes' last days which are described in the text but may be read from Cormack's handwriting on this page.

Chapter IX

Death

Surely their lake was cursed. These last few survivors abandoned it and went to live at the junction of Badger Brook and the Exploits River, one of the caribou's natural crossing points. Traces still remain of their few mamateeks and a large old white pine, which used to be their lookout.

Several years before, other small groups had tried settling on favourable areas along the Exploits. One of these was on a long peninsula of land a little down river from Badger Brook, at Wigwam Brook, a site excavated by archaeologist Ray Leblanc in 1972.

Confluence of Badger Brook and the Exploits.

The old white pine may have been climbed by Shawnadithit to look for caribou crossing.

Log-littered bank of the Exploits River.

Trees grow slowly in Newfoundland. Logging has virtually eliminated white pine. Water levels raised 30 feet have drowned Indian sites on Red Indian Lake.

Badger Brook runs out of a series of upland ponds. The streams which join them flow either north or south according to the season. At high water, the ponds drain into the, then almost uninhabited Hall's Bay area, a good place for shellfish. This route to the sea, rather than the Exploits itself, became the main Beothuk lifeline.

But not for long. Trappers moved into the area and by the end of the harsh winter of 1823, in March, the twenty-five people who were left were all in a sorry state of starvation.

Shawnadithit's fourth sketch tells the painful story graphically. Six of the people died that month and Shanadithit's uncle, Longnon, set out in desperation with his daughter to find shellfish at Badger Bay. Shanadithit has marked the path they took.

When they failed to return, the camp moved; three wigwams containing nineteen people in all. The two remaining members of the missing Lognon's family died in April, leaving seventeen. Shawnadithit, her sister, her mother Doodebewshet, and perhaps one or two male companions (since, at this point, Shawnadithit is quite certain that twelve remained) took off on the same track as her missing uncle and cousin.

They soon found them — shot dead by two furriers named Carey and Adams. Although arraigned, the two were acquitted on grounds of "extenuating circumstances." Just before reaching the sea shore, Shawnadithit's party also ran into some furriers, one of them being William Cull. If there had been male Beothuks in the company, they fell through the ice or were killed. Shawnadithit and her younger sister escaped, but Doodebewshet was taken. Since she was not killed out of hand, she decided to save her daughters from starvation by leading her captors to the place where she knew they would be hiding.

The little family was taken by Peyton to St. John's and there were the subject of a great deal of interest. Rev. William Wilson's book *Newfoundland and its Missionaries*, contains an extract from his journal which poignantly describes part of their time there.

June 24th — Saw the three Indian women in the street. The ladies had dressed them in English garb, but over the dresses they all had on their, to them, indispensable deerskin shawls; and Shawnadithit thinking the long front of her bonnet an unnecessary appendage had torn it off and in its place had decorated her forehead and her arms with tinsel and coloured paper.

They took a few trinkets and a quantity of the fancy paper that is usually wrapped around pieces of linen; but their great selection was pots, kettles, hatchets, hammers, nails and other articles of ironmongery, with which they were loaded, so that they could scarcely walk. It was painful to see the sick woman who, notwithstanding her debility, was determined to have her share in these valuable treasures.

Shawnadithit's sister was the one who was very sick. Soon after the Governor ordered Buchan to return the family to Red Indian Lake to search for any other survivors, Shawnadithit's sister died.

Now there was only Shawnadithit and her old mother. Buchan left them near Red Indian Lake to look for any other Beothuk who might be left alive. In a little boat, Shawnadithit and her mother searched for several months, journeying to every campsite. But no-one was found.

Mrs. Doug Woodman, born on the shores of Red Indian Lake has lived there all her life. She is the unofficial caretaker of and hospitable guide to the Indian sites. She stands in her garden holding the hand of Luba Such.

Doodebewshet had worn herself out. Shawnadithit had to face the fact that her mother was dying and that she would soon be the last of her race. Provisions were low, the summer was nearly over. How could she survive entirely alone? When her mother became unable to travel, they camped on a sandy point and she waited for her mother to die. Shawnadithit cut birchbark from the trees to sew her body in, held her in her dying moments, and sang the People's last lament.

Then she buried her mother in the sand, picked up the last of her provisions and set out for the coast.

Some time later she stumbled out to Notre Dame Bay. She was the last of her people.

The House in St. John's in which Shawnawdithit lived (Roopes) drawn by herself.

Shawnadithit's drawing of where she lived in St. John's.

Under the large house drawn by Shawnadithit is a small one probably drawn by a "white" hand, perhaps by Shawnadithit herself, which is an attempt to use modern perspective. What Shawnadithit has drawn is the "whole" house, not just one point of view of it. The front and back doors are superimposed and the two chimneys are really the front and back views of the same one. Courtesy James P. Howley, The Beothuks or Red Indians.

Strangely enough, public interest in her declined, and she lived in obscurity as a domestic in Peyton's household in Twillingate. It is said that while she was there she was shot at twice by Indian killers. One, Noel Boss, a Métis of English and Micmac background, boasted that he had killed ninety-nine and wished to make her his hundredth.

She seemed to be cheerful except for certain times when she would suddenly walk into the surrounding woods and commune with the spirits of her mother and sister. Returning three days later, she would be laughing about the things that they had told her.

William Epps Cormack, a famous Newfoundland explorer and scholar who had been educated at Edinburgh University, grew interested in the Beothuk and founded the Beothuk Institute for their protection in 1827. Luckily he arranged to have Shawnadithit sent to him in St. John's where he questioned her extensively about her people. He himself had gone on a melancholy expedition to Red Indian Lake to find traces of her people the previous year. He had found many Beothuk campsites, but no trace that they had been occupied for some time.

Shawnadithit, or "Nancy". Portrait by Helen S. Parsons, 1951. Courtesy Newfoundland Museum.

ing him a lock of her hair. She also gave him a piece of quartz and a rounded piece of granite from the shores of Red Indian Lake: two tiny symbols, all that remained of the great territory in which the Beothuk had once prospered.

Soon after, the 29-year-old woman was dead, buried in the Anglican cemetery, the South Side, St. John's. Her grave was lost when the cemetery gave way to a city street.

There is no fitting monument to commemorate the people who originally lived in harmony with the lakes, forests, coasts and animals of Newfoundland. Everything the Beothuk used was made of natural materials and decayed rapidly in Newfoundland soil, leaving only the few scraps we now have. There is a small provincial park on a short stretch of the shore of Red Indian Lake, and some artifacts in the museum at St. John's. And of the People themselves? There is only an uneasy retelling of their story, when the younger generation of Newfoundlanders poses the question: "Whatever happened to the people who lived here first?"

While she was in his home, Shawnadithit developed a great fondness for him and drew for him her story-maps and pictures. From Cormack's few notes, left with the Beothuk Institute, it seems that Shawnadithit also told him about the People's customs and religious beliefs.

Cormack may have been preparing a work for publication but the great bulk of his material — if indeed it ever existed — disappeared. Early in 1829 he had to leave for New Westminster, B.C. and probably took it with him. Perhaps someday his material will be found, either in old family papers in New Westminster, where he died in 1868, or in Edinburgh where he frequently visited, or even in New Zealand, where he went on a colonizing expedition.

At their parting, Shawnadithit, sensing her own approaching death, responded to his kindness by giv-

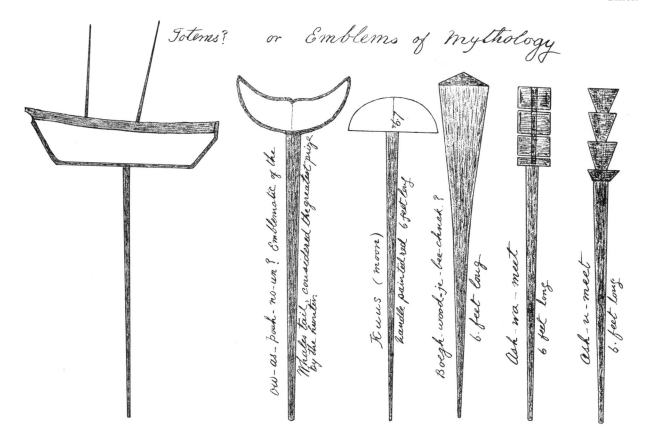

Shawnadithit's drawing of Beothuk ceremonial staffs.

Any further information about the emblems of mythology drawn below were lost when Cormack took his notes with him to New Westminster, B.C. Courtesy James P. Howley, The Beothuks or Red Indians.

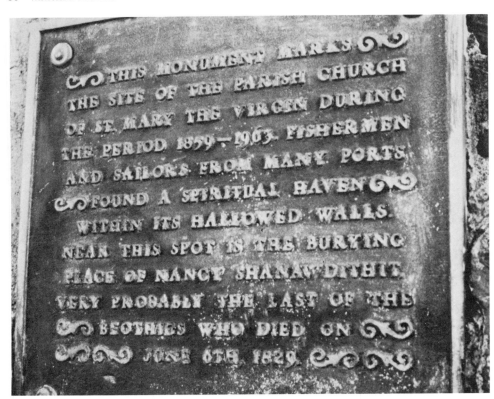

*Shawnadithit's Monument,
St. John's Harbour,
Newfoundland.*

For Further Reading

The books and articles listed below are not a complete list. They are those which will be most helpful for further reading.

Berton, Pierre. *My Country,* M & S, 1976.

Carignan, Paul C. *The Beaches: a Multi-Component Habitation Site in Bonavista Bay.* Mercury Series No. 39, National Museum of Man, 1975.

Carpenter, Edmund. *Eskimo Realities,* Holt, Rinehart, Winston, 1973.

Harp, Elmer Jr. *Cultural Affinities of the Newfoundland Dorset Eskimo.* National Museum of Canada, Bulletin 200.

————. "Late Dorset Eskimo Art from Newfoundland." *Folk* 1969/70, pp. 109-123.

Hewson, John. "Beothuck and Algonkian: Evidence Old and New." *International Journal of American Linguistics,* Vol. 34, Number 2, April '68, pp. 85-93.

Horwood, Harold. "The People Who Were Murdered For Fun." *Maclean's Magazine,* Oct. 1959.

Howley, James P. *The Beothucks or Red Indians.* Cambridge, 1915, and as reprinted and edited by J. G. Bradley, Coles Canadiana, 1974.

Jenness, Diamond. "The Vanished Red Indians of Newfoundland." *Can. Geog. Journal,* Vol. 8, #1, Jan. 1934, pp. 27-32.

Lindsay, Charles. "Was L'Anse aux Meadows a Norse Outpost?" *Canadian Geographical Journal,* Feb./March, 1977, pp. 36-43.

Linnamae, Urve. *The Dorset Culture,* Technical papers of the Newfoundland Museum, No. 1, 1975.

MacLeod, D. "The Archaic in Newfoundland and Labrador." *Ontario Archaeological Society Bulletin,* Feb. 1973, pp. 3-9.

Magnusson, M. and Palsson, H. (ed.). *The Vinland Sagas: The Norse Discovery of America.* Penguin, 1976.

McGhee, Robert. *The Burial at L'Anse-Amour.* National Museum of Man, Ottawa, 1976.

McGhee, R. and Tuck, J. "Did the Medieval Irish Visit Newfoundland." *Canadian Geographical Journal,* June/July, 1977, pp. 66-73.

Speck, Frank G. *Beothuk and Micmac.* New York: Museum of the American Indian Foundation, 1922.

Such, Peter. *Riverrun,* Clarke, Irwin, 1973.

Tuck, James A. *Newfoundland and Labrador Prehistory.* National Museum of Man, Ottawa, 1976.

Glossary

Adze:

A specialized wood-working tool that is attached to a handle at a right angle, in the same manner as a hoe.

Algonkian, Indian:

A widespread language family that includes the Micmac and Malecite of the Atlantic provinces, and the Montagnais, Cree, Algonkin and Ojibwa of the Canadian Shield.

Amulet:

An ornament worn as a charm to bring the wearer good luck. Usually highly stylized representations of animals or birds, to be attached to hunting weapons.

Anthropology, Anthropologist:

The science of man in relation to physical character, distribution, origin and distribution of race, environmental and social relations, and culture. One who practises this science.

Archaeology:

The study of ancient peoples, often by excavation of their former habitations or burial grounds.

Archaic, Archaic Peoples:

A term used to describe an ancient hunting, fishing and gathering stage of culture in eastern North America. This period is characterized by ground slate and chipped flint tools, and the extensive use of red ochre in burials. The development of pottery and weaving skills mark the end of the Archaic period.

Awl:

A sharply pointed tool, usually made from bone, which was used for punching holes in leather, birchbark or other materials in preparation for their use.

Canadian Shield:

A very ancient, stable landmass of mostly precambrian rock which runs in a horseshoe shape around Hudson's Bay, through Labrador, Quebec and Ontario, and the northern parts of Manitoba.

Carbon 14 Test (Radioactive dating):

A dating method for plant and animal matter which relies upon their absorption of carbon during their lifetimes. After the death of the organism, the radioactive isotope (carbon 14) begins to dissipate at a rate which can be accurately measured. The amount of this isotope present in organic material is a reliable indicator of the time that has elapsed since its death.

Dorset Culture, Dorset Eskimos:

A regional development of the earliest Eskimo people to occupy the Arctic, this culture was found in the central and eastern Arctic as far east as Greenland. It reached its furthest territorial extension about 2000 B.C., but was gradually replaced from 1000 A.D. by the Thule Eskimos.

Effigy:

A sculptured or pictured likeness of a human form, person or god.

Flint:

A very hard silica rock, usually gray, which produces sparks when struck against another piece of flint or against steel, and thus was commonly used to ignite fires. It also flakes with sharp edges when split and so can be shaped into tools.

Housepit:

A depression in the ground where a semi-subterranean house once stood. Housepits have been found from Dorset and Beothuk cultures in Newfoundland.

Linguistics:

The study of human speech, including the origin, structure and modification of language or languages.

Liverpool Manuscript:

Discovered by Nimshe Crewe, former Newfoundland archivist, this manuscript contains the report of Magistrate John Bland about the relations of the Beothuks and white settlers of the Twillingate area. Field notes for it appear to have been written by one G. C. Pulling.

Maritime Archaic, Maritime Archaic Peoples:

An archaic culture group who lived mostly on the coasts 7500 to 3000 years ago. Known to have inhabited Labrador, Newfoundland, the Maritimes and New England, these people may also have flourished on the Northwest Pacific coasts. They survived until recently in isolated parts of Newfoundland.

Micmac:

A tribe of Algonkian-speaking Indians found mainly in Nova Scotia and parts of New Brunswick.

Midden:

An accumulation of refuse about a dwelling place; a refuse heap marking the site of a primitive habitation.

Montagnais:

An Algonkian-speaking group living in the Quebec - Labrador peninsula. These people were closely related to the Naskapi.

Mound, Burial Mound:

An artificial hill of earth placed over a gravesite, often capped with large stones.

Naskapi:

An Algonkian-speaking tribe, mostly caribou hunters, neighbours of the Montagnais on the north shore of the Gulf of St. Lawrence.

Nomad, Nomadic:

One of a people or tribe that has no fixed dwelling place, but wanders from one area to another, often in a regular yearly round.

Norse, Norse Sagas:

Of or pertaining to ancient Scandinavia, or the language of its inhabitants. The Norse Sagas were long epic poems about exploration and settlement. Two Sagas relate to the exploration of North America. The earliest and most reliable is the "Graenlendinga" Saga. The second is "Eirik's Saga".

Paint-Stones:

Stones used as pots in which to mix pigments.

Paleo:

Very early, the furthest distant in time. Of or pertaining to ancient human cultures characterized by their use of rough or chipped stone implements.

Paleo-Eskimo:

The name given to a number of cultures which occupied the Canadian Arctic between 4 000 and 1 000 years ago.

Paleo-Indian:

The earliest recognizable Indian culture in North America, dating from perhaps 30 000 to 9 000 years ago.

Pestle:

A tool used to pound or grind material, usually grain, especially in a mortar. A mortar was usually made of a slab of granite or other hard rock that became hollowed out from continual use.

Projectile point:

An artifact, pointed at one end, and attached to a spear, dart or arrow at the opposite end.

Ramah Chert:

A distinctive, translucent grey silicate with a rounded granular surface texture. It occurs only in northern Labrador but has been found in widely scattered archaeological sites throughout North America.

Red Ochre:

A natural pigment (a hydrated oxide of iron) widely used by Native cultures for painting objects, and in ritual sprinkling of the bodies of the dead.

Shaman:

An individual who possesses recognized magical powers. The religion of the Ural-Altaic peoples of northern Asia, Europe and North America centres on the Shaman's intercession in the spirit world on behalf of the people.

Skraelings:

The name given by the Norse to various New World peoples; in Newfoundland it may have referred to the Beothuk, Naskapi or Eskimos.

Soapstone:

Steatite, a soft stone with a soapy texture found widely in the Canadian Arctic and Newfoundland. It is used for making cooking vessels, oil lamps, and carving sculptures.

Thule Eskimos:

People of the Thule culture who migrated out of Alaska about 900 A.D. and soon occupied nearly all of the Canadian Arctic, Labrador, Greenland and the coast of Quebec, replacing the earlier Dorset migration. The Inuit of today are their direct descendents.

Toggle, Toggling Harpoon head:

A detachable weapon, the strength of which derives from its function of "toggling" or turning in the wound. It is attached to the shaft by a line from the centre of the tip.

Vineland, Vinland Sagas:

See Norse.

Weir:

A construction of stone or wood which stands in the water and channels fish so that they can be readily caught.

Index